The Dead-End Road Devotional

Fishing for Principles and Truths on Life's Journey

The People Pastor

Bill Fix

Dedication

I dedicate this book to my Savior, Jesus Christ, for giving me a full and abundant life. Also, in loving memory of my dad and mom, Tony and Vadna Fix. Dad had a sixth-grade education, with a Ph.D. in common sense, and Mom had a fourth-grade education with a doctorate in encouragement and motivation. Together they were an excellent team. They taught me principles that continue to guide my life today. Our home was full of encouragement, warmth, love, humor, and joy. Both my parents were hard-working, kind, gentle, wise, and fun. When they went to heaven to be with Jesus, they left behind an incredible and exemplary legacy.

With the love and support of my gorgeous wife, Dottie, our two beautiful daughters, Leona and Lynnette, and their two amazing husbands, Toby and Jason, I was encouraged to write *The Dead-End Road Devotional*. My grandchildren, Lydia, Joel, Lucy and Jerod, participated in several conversations that helped me think through a few details for the book. I love and appreciate them all, very much.

I want to also thank my siblings: Tom, Jim, Joan, and the late Harry; and their spouses and families for their love and support over the years. Their support has indeed helped to make sweet memories of home.

With Love,

Bill Fix, The People Pastor

Table of Contents

Introduction

This book was born from classic childhood memories of fishing with my Dad. The Dead-End Road was an extraordinary place where Dad and I fished. It's on the Olentangy River between Delaware and Marion, Ohio, where the road ended, and a journey began.

We bonded at this place and shared experiences that brought us together in a close and binding relationship. Dad taught me to fish and became a model of how a father is to love his children. Fishing quickly became my favorite activity to do with him. Not only is the Dead-End Road a great memory but the adventures we shared there were epic.

I was five years old when this adventure began, but many of the memories I have of Dad and this place I will never forget. My legs were little, and my body frail, but my energy level was off the charts, especially when I was with Dad at the Dead-End Road. To navigate some of the trails, we had to climb over fallen trees and huge rocks, which was a challenge. Dad had to watch me closely because with him by my side, I believed I could do anything.

As time went on, I learned many valuable lessons from Dad, and became a pretty good fisherman. Today, the times we shared then have become very precious to me. His commitment to taking me fishing was not financially expensive thing for him. Dad's most significant investment was with his time. And time was the investment that I valued the most. I cherish these memories of a kind and generous father who invested his time teaching me principles and truths about life. This book reflects how these experiences have impacted my life.

Back then, there was no place I'd rather be than fishing with Dad, and it was always a special treat when Mom went along. When I became a dad, there was nothing more enjoyable than experiencing life with our daughters, Leona and Lynnette, and my wife and their mother, Dottie. The most valuable investment I've made has not been in dollars but in spending time together.

I hope you enjoy reading *The Dead-End Road Devotional* as much as I have enjoyed writing it. As you turn the pages, please remember that the simplest truths are always the most profound, and what I share in this book are simple truths. My prayer is for *The Dead-End Road Devotional* to make you think and reflect upon life. May the thoughts and experiences shared in this devotional book be helpful and have a positive effect on you, your life, and your future. Journey on!

The People Pastor, Bill Fix

Acknowledgments

With the support of an excellent launch team, I moved forward with writing *The Dead-End Road Devotional*. The team prayed for me and encouraged and aided me throughout my concentrated effort to write this book during August 2019. They provided suggestions and comments throughout the process and I am grateful for every one of them. A book could be written about each person on the team and I genuinely love them all.

Bill Fix, The People Pastor

The Book Launch Team

*Diana Andrews   *Nelson & Camille Blount
*Melisa Byars   *John & Heather Cabanaw
*Sharon Cabanaw   *Bob England
*Marianne Fitzpatrick   *Jim & Carol Fix
*Tony & Mo Fix   *Tammy Hamann Salazar
*Wes & Christin Hardin   *Marion Hartley
*Joel Hunt   *Leona & Toby Hunt
*Lydia Hunt   *Stephanie Jackson
*Richard Jewett   *Dave & Dorothy Mathis
*Adam & Jessica O'Neil   *Paul & *Leah O'Neil
*Betty Rosenberger   *Scott & Gail Smith
*Jerod Snyder   *Lucy Snyder
*Lynnette & Jason Snyder   *Dorothy Winbigler Fix
*Denise & Bud Wylie

*Denotes direct input into the book
(list continues on the next page)

Mary Ann Abraham	Dave & Lois Anderson
Glen Bert	Jimmy & Jeannette Bolton
Simone Calvas	Kim Carter
Ed Cavendar	Amber Duffy
Bob Eaton	Gary Goodsell
Linda & Terry Haugh	Carol Hicks
Dorothy Hodges	Rose Marie Johnson
Susan Kozak	Irene Love
Amber Mahaffey	Eric & April Martin
David Masse	Harry & Ann Matthews
Bob & Cheryl McFarlane	Christina Moore
Faye Morocca	Kay & Mark Morton
Bob & Marge O'Neil	Dan & Hope Owsley
Anita Polymeneas	Sandy Pratt
Herbert & Sarah Rowsey	Scott Smith, Jr.
Lynnette & Joe Sobicinski	Hank Sower
Ron & Margie Sutton	Jesse Washington
Craig Watson	Paul J. Weber
Sue Westphal Williams	Lynne & George Williams
Marie Wilson	Beth Zellner

Chapter One

Roads Might End, but the Journey Continues

God is the giver of eternal hope. Once you receive it, you will be forever changed. My prayer is for you to find the Father God of hope.

May the God of hope fill you with all joy and peace as you trust in him, so that you may overflow with hope by the power of the Holy Spirit. [Romans 15:13]

What would you call a road that suddenly ends at a cliff's edge, twenty-five feet above the Olentangy River? Dad and I called it The Dead-End Road, where the road ends, and the journey begins.

An Invitation Linked to Hope

The journey started with an invitation to go fishing with my Dad. He'd invited me to experience my first fishing trip with him that coming Saturday. I had Dad's promise and knew the precise day when this event would happen. Although I didn't have any inkling about what awaited me or all the adventure in store for me, I can tell you that the anticipation grew as the day approached.

Invitations or exciting plans have always been a trigger that released something inside of me. I can't explain what happens, but as I dwell upon the plans, I feel something in my heart. The anticipation begins to replay over and over again and hope is born and begins to grow. I started calling this reaction the *hope factor* in my life.

> The hope factor awakens me physically and mentally.

It gives me energy and excitement and bubbles up inside me. Norman Vincent Peale wrote about this in his book, *The Power of Positive Thinking*. At five years old, I learned that positive thinking had power. The fishing trip was undoubtedly a decisive moment in my life. I began thinking about it continually. Fishing with Dad was a good thought, and it was feeding my hope factor. Hope is something that gets me up in the morning, and because I have faith that what I hope for will happen, hope grows.

Now faith is the substance of things hoped for, the evidence of things not seen. [Hebrews 11:1, KJV]

At a young age, I understood life could hurt when I'm not included or don't receive an invitation.

> **Life could hurt when I'm not included or don't receive an invitation.**

I knew what it felt like to see Dad load up the car with fishing poles and equipment to take my older brothers fishing without me. It had happened many times, and they would come back with all kinds of exciting stories. I wanted to go along, but Dad said I was too young. At that point, the reason I couldn't go didn't matter much to me. Exclusion had a tremendous sting, and was no fun at all.

I knew how it felt to be left out, and experiencing that has made me a better person and more aware of others who might be feeling left out.

I was thin, had red hair and freckles and was very short. My eyes were bright blue and my complexion fair. I had tremendous energy and was in constant motion. I seldom stopped running. Not only was my body in continuous motion, but my mouth never stopped. It was natural for me to be curious about things and ask a lot of questions. I began asking questions when I woke up in the morning and continued until I fell asleep at night.

I learned that if I didn't ask, I would never know.

And if I asked politely and often enough, I would eventually receive an answer. I learned that by asking the right questions, I would gain tremendous knowledge and details. Asking questions and talking with others about the upcoming fishing trip on Saturday helped to fill in more details. These specifics caused my hope and expectation to grow.

> If I didn't ask, I would never know.

The more I learned about the trip, the more excited I became. I found out I would have my very own fishing pole. I learned that Dad and I were going to collect nightcrawlers the night before the trip. Mom told me we would be taking a lunch complete with snacks that I'd enjoy. These details caused my expectations for the journey to increase and my hope to intensify.

We talked about the trip often. Much of the joy of my experiences happened before the event, during the planning. Hope needed to grow as the fishing day approached because if hope stagnated, it would vanish. Hope was living in me as we were preparing for this fishing trip. It was a living hope—it grew and matured.

> If we fail to renew hope, it expires.

Hope is like a crescendo in music, getting bigger and bigger until its climax becomes a reality.

That is how I felt during the week as I waited for the big fishing day to arrive.

I did not have a calendar back then, but I understood how long a week was. I knew that Saturday was coming up real soon. Every day when I got up to have breakfast, I asked the same question: Is this Saturday? Hope had filled me with an indescribable joy. When I grew old enough to have and understand calendars, I grew to love them and still do today. They are not only a scheduling and tracking tool, but they document hopes and expectations as well.

My calendar contains opportunities, experiences, desires, and dreams. When I cunduct pre-marriage counseling, I teach the calendar hope-factor. I think every person should have something on their calendar that they're hoping to do. Previously, I had been looking forward to taking the month of August to write this book while in Florida. Writing plans were on my calendar for about a year, and my wife and I shared in the exciting preparations to make it happen. My future with the Lord's leading has built-in hope, with plans, opportunities, and celebrations.

> Just looking at my hope-filled calendar is exciting to me.

The calendar hope-factor means something exciting will always be on the calendar. Over the course of many years, my hope-filled schedule has been so encouraging. Recently, I added a trip to Kansas in late December and a trip back to Florida in July.

Not only can I look ahead at what I hope to do, but I can look back and see how God has been my helper and how He has blessed my life. Recently, I looked back at an awesome event at which I had the privilege of giving the invocation for a multicampus community college graduation at Ford Field. It was a thrill to be a part of this event when two thousand students received their diplomas. It was exciting and tremendously humbling to glance up at the jumbotron and see The People Pastor inviting the graduates and their guests to pray. My calendar allows me to look forward with hope and to look back at fond memories.

I often say, "I am filled up with hope." Years ago as a young boy, hope and expectation grew as the countdown to the fishing day progressed. I can look back to a time when I was only five years old and thank God for that experience. Hope has always been a powerful fuel to wake me up in the morning and keep me going throughout my day. I expect life to be productive and fulfilling, and it is.

Unfortunately, unless hope culminates with something tangible, it becomes a shattered dream. I can think of several shattered dreams in my life, but I choose not to dwell on them. For some, shattered dreams become a constant diet. Their hope invariably ends in nothing which is a tragic and devastating experience. Disappointment, sadness, and depression often follow.

Hope can be powerful in a positive way, and hope canceled can be powerful in a negative way. At the root of people's chronic sadness and depression is the constant heartache of shattered hope. Hope stops working as a power source when faith in the future disappears.

Hope and anticipation occur before an event. During this time, preparation and readiness need to take place. Part of getting ready for our fishing trip was gathering nightcrawlers the night before we planned to go. Dad had held a flashlight in one hand and snatched the nightcrawlers with the other. He was very good at it. I'd tried it and only managed to snatch half a nightcrawler. Outside at night with Dad, hunting for nightcrawlers became an adventure in itself. My dream of fishing with Dad had seemed to get even better as we'd prepared for the trip.

Finally, the fishing day arrived, and as Dad drank a cup of coffee, I hurriedly ate my breakfast. I was so full of hope, that I wasn't very hungry. We packed the family car, and for the first time in my life, I jumped into the front seat beside Dad. We stopped at the bait shop to buy some minnows. There must have been a million minnows in the tank. Dad had bought two dozen, but it looked like a hundred. My hope had begun maturing into reality even before we'd arrived at the river.

A Dead-End Road Can Be a Blessing

As we neared our destination, I stood on the front seat as Dad drove down a bumpy road. Suddenly, we came to a massive barrier across the road and a big red sign. Dad read the sign out loud. "Stop! Bridge Out, Road Ends!" The road ended at a cliff, and about twenty-five feet below was the Olentangy River. This place was frequently called the Dead-End Road.

I have to admit, when I saw that barrier across the road, my heart sank. Dad had assured me that even though the road ended, our excellent fishing adventure was just beginning. Since that day, I haven't forgotten how my heart sunk when I'd first seen the road's end. I'd been afraid the fishing trip would end also.

Often, when a road I'm travelling suddenly ends, my heart sinks, fear sets in, and hope seems to evaporate. Dead-end roads appear to be final. When I look toward the horizon, I usually do not see the stop sign. When it suddenly appears, I slam on the brakes and heaviness seems to permeate my soul. I feel a sudden disappointment, like the initial reaction I had when I was with Dad that day. Despair can steal away my joy, at least for the moment.

Not until I look back and reflect on these experiences do I see how dead-end roads can be real blessings. They become teachable moments, learning experiences, a push in the right direction, and a launch to a new horizon. Experience has taught me that dead-end roads are not dead, and certainly not the end. In every instance so far, when one road ended, God helped me find a new and often better road to travel. Satan would have me think it was over, and that I've failed, but in truth, the journey continued.

> It is always easier to look back and thank God for dead-end road experiences than it is to thank Him at the moment the road ends.

At that first dead-end road, I discovered a great place to fish. My initial reaction is almost always immediate panic. Sometimes it's hard to shake feelings of failure. I need time to stop, reflect, and assess what just happened and where I am in life. A dead end often means delay, but it rarely means defeat.

I used to think these events were the work of some enemy. Things would be going great and then all of a sudden, they'd blow up. I felt like a loving God wouldn't do that. I have grown to believe these experiences were not the work of the Devil, but quite the opposite. God often brings me to that dead end. He suddenly slams a door shut so that I can no longer go that direction. God knows this is the only way to convince me to do something different.

I've never been a quitter at anything, but I have been forced to quit at times. God's direction is what I pray for, and I wouldn't want it any other way.

> I think of situations when I was forced to quit as God's way of leading me to different places.

At that first dead-end road, I trusted Dad. What else could I do? Yell, scream, and throw a fit? What good would that have done? Dad was in control of the situation. Since then, I have learned to react differently. Although I initially panic, I know it is time to trust my heavenly Father. He is in control. What else can I do? Yell, scream, throw a fit? What good would that do? Those who decide to throw fits when a road ends seldom make things better. Throwing a fit usually makes things worse. Trusting God is a better plan.

At the Dead-End Road, the isolation from problems and chaos was amazing but I was not alone. Dad was there. He had a plan, and although I was not in control, Dad was. As a control freak, I dislike not being in control, but most of life is like that—beyond our control. I have taken dead ends personally. I have punished myself with the thought that each dead end is entirely my fault. I continue to learn not to think that way, but trust God instead.

God continues to teach me that all earthly roads we travel on eventually end.

> All earthly roads we travel on eventually end.

Sometimes the ending is predictable and expected, and other times, the ending is unexpected and scary. Instead of making accusations and pointing my finger at myself or others, I need to point it toward the next steps in the journey of life. I have been working on putting that into practice.

At every dead end, I can trust my heavenly Father. Trusting God does not make the journey easy, but it keeps me moving. Dead ends are places where I should look to Him for guidance. "What now?" What's next? If every earthly road ends, we must trust that God will lead us to our next path. With God leading, the journey will be fruitful.

It is good to ponder on what we believe will happen when that future day comes—the day we breathe our last earthly breath. As a Christian, I believe the journey will not be over. Christians believe in eternal life. A side to life beyond the grave that theologians, teachers and preachers don't teach much about relates to our legacy which also lives on. When others mention our name after we are gone, or remember what we've taught them, or do what they've seen us do, or believe what we believe, our legacy—good or bad—lives on. When we leave this Earth, what we've built into others' lives will continue to live in them. What we've given away, invested in others, and stood for, along with the lives that have been influenced by our love, principles, and character lives on. Hopefully, people will remember Christ in me and you. Legacies continue until a generation fails to pass it on. But for those who believe in Jesus, our eternity awaits. Our road here on Earth may end, but the journey continues and is part of the eternal quest.

Discussion Questions

1. Dad taught me the value of being filled with hope. What plans on your calendar are you looking forward to with expectation and hope?
2. Dad taught me the journey is worth the wait. With the right preparation, the wait becomes an adventure. What type of preparation is required for some of the events on your calendar?
3. How can preparation be a journey in itself?

4. Dad allowed me to annoy him with all kinds of questions as the fishing day approached. When was the last time you excitedly went to the Father with questions about your future hopes?
5. Have you or someone you love come to a dead end along life's journey? What's next?
6. What do you think this fishing trip cost my Dad? Answer: Not much, but I will remember it forever. Have you ever thought that parenting was expensive? What's more important: the expense or the relationship?
7. When you breathe your final breath, what legacy do you think you will leave behind? Have you thought about how valuable, glorious and wonderful eternity in heaven will be?

Prayer

Thank you, Father for my hope in Jesus. You are an awesome God that I can trust and come to with endless chatter. You listen as I talk to you about everything. You know all about my life and the people I love. I realize that you are in control of all things and thank you. I trust and love you. Help me cling to my faith when I forget my hope is in Jesus. Help me to remember that dead-end roads are often the result of you guiding me in another direction that will eventually lead me to heaven. Help me to have hope, share hope, and give hope to those around me. I pray this in the mighty name of Jesus. Amen.

Launch Team Comments

I loved my job as Assistant Principal. I loved the children, the faculty and other staff members. My career was rewarding, fruitful, and fulfilling. When the administration of the school district changed, the direction of the new administration was contrary to my life principles. I prayed and asked God to help me decide what to do. I decided to resign from the job I loved. My heart broke. During the process, I received an offer for a job that helps teachers across the nation. God retooled me as I moved into the new position. Today, I once again feel the fulfillment of making a positive difference in the education of children. L.F.H.

I thought my journey ended after what happened to me as a child and teenager. I tried ending my journey, but God had other plans. I met my husband and then found the Lord in August of 1972. The trajectory of my life immediately changed, and since that time, I have been serving the Lord. D.W.F.

God closed the door (the road ended) on a radio program I was running at a local station. It was my dream job. The road ended rather abruptly. On one particular Saturday, I was told that I would push through the hard place. The next Saturday as I was closing the door to leave, I was told, "You won't be coming back." It was the last program at the station. God closed the program out just the way I would have wanted it to close had I known it was the last show. He led me into something new that I was not good at and apart from my passion of being around Christian authors. He was faithful to bring me through the transition. I am grateful I went out on a positive note. D.W.

When Light and Life Christian School closed, it was more than the ending of a job to me. A part of my life was ending as well. I attended Light and Life from pre-school through high school and then worked at my first post-college job there. That school was involved in seventeen years of my life. That's half of my life right now. I still resent the school closure. The closure of the school positively moved me forward. Were it not for the closure, I would have never gone to law school, met my wife, moved to Florida, started my law firm, or be where I am now. When the school doors closed, it forced me out of my comfort zone—not because I didn't have a job, as I could have gotten a job elsewhere—but because it ended a period of my life and I needed to move on. When the school closed, it forced me to grow and seek out my potential. A.O.

Chapter Two

The High Path of Contemplation

I was glad that jumping off the cliff was not the only way to the river. Although a sudden leap would have taken me there, the sudden stop could have ended this incredible journey. We have all jumped off figurative cliffs, and we know it generally does not end well. Friends have ended their life because all they could see was the dead end. They could not see the journey that could have been theirs. This was especially sad because they'd forgotten or didn't know what I know: roads end but journeys do not.

To get to the river from the road, only one way was safe. A series of paths meandered along the banks of the Olentangy River. One of the three types of paths was the high, wide, and easy path. Another was the path in between—the transition path. It was steep, could be dangerous and was usually slippery. The river path, the one closest to the water, was my favorite. It was the path of action. The path of action was the lowest, most active, and most dangerous because it was closest to river activities.

The high path of contemplation is not the only place to encounter God, but it is one of the most significant places at which to get close to Him. My prayer is that the chaos of life will not crowd out times for you to go to the mountain—the high path—and meet with an unhurried, non-stressed-out God. Jesus said that His yoke is easy and his burden, light. That is why we need a high path so much. We have a great need for our burdens to be lifted and to experience Jesus's easy yoke and light burden.

15When Moses went up on the mountain, the cloud covered it, 16and the glory of the LORD settled on Mount Sinai. For six days the cloud covered the mountain, and on the seventh

*day the LORD called to Moses from within the cloud. 17To the
Israelites the glory of the LORD looked like a consuming fire
on top of the mountain. 18Then Moses entered the cloud as
he went on up the mountain. And he stayed on the mountain
forty days and forty nights. [Exodus 24:15-18]*

Someone Is in Control

When the road ended, the journey seemed to have ended
too. But it hadn't. My dad had control of this situation. He had
been there before with my three brothers and knew what he was
doing. Dad would show me what was next on this journey. He'd
intended to bring me to the Dead-End Road to lead me on an
incredible journey.

After he'd parked the car, we unloaded the trunk and began
what appeared might be a lengthy hike to the river. Dad was in
the lead, and when we first stepped onto the path, I felt like we
were in a jungle or wilderness because it was so unfamiliar. I
don't think I'd ever been on a path like this before. I loved it and
followed him as he'd told me to do.

The first path was easy walking, and I was glad. Dad
seemed to be moving very quickly. I began to realize that for
every step he took, I had to take two or three steps. If he had
decided to walk fast, I would have been running. I loved this
path though; I could see a very long way ahead. At times I was
afraid while in the shadows, but felt great comfort knowing Dad
was there with a plan and experience enough to know what he
was doing. He was in control.

We'd been loaded down with everything Dad had thought
we might need. I carried all I could bear, and dad had the rest.
We took lawn chairs, packed lunches, a thermos bottle of coffee,
fishing poles, a tackle box, a can of nightcrawlers, and a
minnow bucket; we brought a lot of equipment.

The first path we traveled was high above the river. That one had no low hanging branches or hard to navigate obstacles in our way. The path was wide and well-traveled. We had time to look around, enjoy the view, and think about how much fun we were going to have fishing. We'd taken the high path to contemplate where we were and where we were going. We had time to examine our choices, choose our next path, and enjoy not having to struggle with weeds and branches as we walked.

Many Choices on the High Path

In life, the high path of contemplation is both delightfully rewarding and necessary. We crave this path when the burdens are heavy and the nights become sleepless. When our plate is full and running over with obligations, responsibilities, expectations, and a long "to-do" list, the high path is where we long to be. It's a path for thinking things through and figuring out the complexities of life. When I feel like I cannot bear one more thing, this is the path I desire to find. It's the only path where I can be alone with the Father.

For the past thirty-eight years, I have served at churches as a lead pastor. At times, I've felt overwhelmed and on the brink of burn-out. I've often needed to transition to the high path of contemplation to regain perspective, begin to prioritize, renew my strength, and solve problems I was facing. I knew I couldn't continue at the same pace.

> When I began to feel like a Human Doer instead of a Human Being, I knew I needed to find the high path.

A Human Doer puts the emphasis on completing projects and has a hard time accepting change. A Human

Being enjoys the process and welcomes necessary change. The Doer exists and the Being lives.

I always did my best to respond to others' needs. At various times during my ministry, I have realized that more needs existed than I could handle. I did not have enough time or enough resources to meet the needs of everyone. I understood a tremendous biblical truth one day: The Bible does not say, "Pastor Bill will meet all your needs." The Bible says:

And my God will meet all your needs according to the riches of his glory in Christ Jesus. [Philippians 4:19]

Many people carry very heavy loads: aging family members; the passing of loved ones; financial chaos; job loss; a sick child; cancer; turmoil; drama; relationship issues; divorce; addiction; and the list goes on. A combination of issues like these can be overwhelming for any one of us. When we become stressed out about everything, we need the high path of contemplation. Some people call this "alone time" or "time alone with God." Whatever we call it, we need it.

The high path gives us time to think through the issues. On the high path, we have the opportunity to step back and analyze problems and discover solutions and next steps. It is on the high path where we can regain our strength and perspective.

Many times I need to pray and think. I need to rest, prioritize, and get my head on straight. It is during these times that I long for the high path of contemplation. God designed this path for us. We can get close to Him and sense His presence on this path. The high path has many advantages, but these advantages are null and void unless we follow through and take the next steps as God directs.

As we walked the high path that day, many choices were available which Dad had seemed to ignore. Numerous paths led to the river and a few led away from the river. We walked right by all of these. He was focused and knew where he wanted to take me, so I just followed.

The path of contemplation is the most comfortable path there is. It's easy to remain on this path, but God does not want us to stay here. This path is designed for decision making, discovering solutions to problems, choosing a new direction or priority, and then transitioning to take action and accomplish something.

My cousin Marion lives in the Philippines. After traveling the path of contemplation, he decisively transitioned from easy street and retirement in the United States to a foreign mission. God is using him in a magnificent Christian work. He realized that retirement was no excuse to be stagnant in service for the Lord. While on the path of contemplation, Marion chose to live out his faith. Today, he feeds thousands of starving children living on the streets of the Philippines.

Most people fail to ask the most critical question on the road of contemplation: How can I best glorify God with my life right now? Like my cousin Marion, we should ask it of ourselves—not only at retirement but throughout our lives. Thank God the path of contemplation—a place where God can help us make decisions—exists. The opportunities are many and the choices are innumerable, and we all need to choose a path where we can best bring glory to God.

In the Bible, Moses met with God on a mountain. To be in the presence of the glory of God was a moment of clarity for Moses. God revealed what He wanted Moses to do, Moses obeyed God, and great things resulted.

Likewise, Jesus went up to a mountain to be with the Father in prayer.

One of those days Jesus went out to a mountainside to pray, and spent the night praying to God. [Luke 6:12]

The same can be true for all of us. The mountain or high path becomes a place where life is slow enough to draw near to God, pray and ask for His help. It is a place to get away from challenging issues and obstacles. Taking this high path is like being on the mountain with God.

Real Truths About the High Path

The high path can become a comfort zone. We often want to stay there, or figuratively, "camp out." After all, it is the easy path.

As Dad and I walked on the high path, I discovered it was well traveled with no low limbs or obstacles of any kind. Yet, the danger in staying on that path for too long meant I wouldn't do any fishing. I couldn't cast my line into the water or catch a single fish from the high path. I hadn't been brought to that place to stay but to discover a suitable transition path down to the river.

Interestingly, the high path followed the river, but it never led to the river. On the high path, I could see the river and talk about fishing in the river, but could never fish the river from it directly. I could only contemplate what it would be like. To fish, we needed to get to the river. To experience what we had previously contemplated, we needed to leave the high path of contemplation and transition to the action.

> The high path followed the river, but it never led to the river.

Dad didn't bring me to the fishing spot to be a spectator. At some point, he planned on helping me to descend and do what we were there to do.

I've learned of at least five reasons why we needed to descend from the high path of contemplation:

- We were there to fish and needed to leave that path to do so.
- I had much to learn about fishing and couldn't learn these things from the high path. Learning through action was necessary.
- Dad needed to descend to teach what he knew.
- Simply talking about what we were there to do and not doing it would have made us hypocrites.
- As a child, I'd been watching and following Dad. If he hadn't taught me to fish, I would have lost respect for him.

Dad didn't just talk about fishing; we went fishing. As a result of his follow-through, I learned to love fishing and gained tremendous respect for my dad.

Today, I never travel on the high path to deal with the issues of life, but to understand them. After my thinking becomes clear, I transition from the high path and do what God has in store for me to do. When the time comes to catch the fish and do the work, we can't do that from the high path. Although we need the high path of contemplation, we should not plan to stay on it.

An old Christian saying assures us, "If God brings you to it, He will lead you through it." This means in challenging times, God will help us. I'm glad that God doesn't just bring us *to* these challenges. He also leads us *through* them. We will accomplish things of great significance when we follow where the Lord leads.

> If God brings you to it, He will lead you through it.

Discussion Questions

1. Think about the high path of contemplation. When do you feel the need to travel the high path? Do you think the path of contemplation is something we seek or something provided by God?

2. Describe a time when you were so overwhelmed that you longed for the high path of contemplation.
3. Describe a time when you were *on* the high path. Were you able to get close to God? Were you able to release your anxieties?
4. How can the high path become a comfort zone? What would persuade you to come down from a place where you felt great comfort?
5. If we don't realize when it is time to transition from the high path, what do you think God will do? Has He ever done that for you?
6. Are there any dangers in trying to walk on the high path?
7. How do you know when it is time to transition and change paths? Do you believe you are on the path that God wants you on right now?

Prayer

Father in heaven, I thank you for the high path. I often long for a time away from the chaos of life to draw near to you and reflect on the journey my life is taking. Thank you for being there and leading me through some really difficult times. I pray that this chapter will resonate with the people who read it. I pray they will understand the importance of the high path and the equal importance of transitioning from it. I appreciate the experiences I had with my earthly Dad. He taught me more than I'd ever comprehended as a child. Help me, Father, to be a blessing to others and always give You glory. Forgive me when I've been too stubborn to transition from the high path, and you've had to kick me off the path I was traveling. I don't always know what you want me to do. At times I am a slow learner. Thank you for my fishing days with Dad. You have continued to teach me much more about walking with and following you. Thank you for being patient with me and guiding me. Please continue to show me your will in my life. I pray this in Jesus's name. Amen.

Launch Team Comments

This chapter got me thinking the high and wide path is where we can become comfortable and content. We make many decisions but not always wise decisions. Our focus is not always on the Lord or working for the Lord, but on ourselves, satisfying our human nature and desires. G.S.

My husband and I desired to have a child, but for some reason, I was unable to get pregnant. The anxiety and stress associated with not being able to become pregnant had me in tears. That was a lot to handle. My husband, Paul, and I decided to look at the adoption option. When I began to relax and trust God for our future, an amazing miracle happened. I became pregnant then delivered our son in January 1993. S.C.

The high path allows you to see your situation from a completely different perspective. My mother had only fished from the shore of a peninsula; she had done that all of her life. I was so glad I was able to take my mother out on my boat. We went out from the peninsula and away from the shoreline where she had always fished. She commented on how different things looked from that perspective. The high path gives those who travel it a different, more reflective perspective. R.J.

Chapter Three
The Path of Transition

Transition is necessary as the environment, our culture, and the world we live in continually changes. Change is inevitable, and we must transition or be left behind. While we transition to new technologies, new cultures, and new opportunities, we still need to maintain some steadfast principles, character traits, and beliefs that do *not* change. I call these things the Principles of Prior Choice. No matter what happens, I will believe and stand by these things. I choose to be kind, respectful, honest, generous, inclusive, and encouraging in all things and all circumstances. Clinging to our principles of prior choice is especially essential in times of transition. They should be our guide, regardless of what changes or what happens.

> *11For I know the plans I have for you, declares the LORD, plans to prosper you and not to harm you, plans to give you hope and a future. 12Then you will call on me and come and pray to me, and I will listen to you. 13You will seek me and find me when you seek me with all your heart. [Jeremiah 29:11-13]*

We Had to Get to the River

Dad and I were in stride on the high road. I took two or three steps for every one of Dad's. Suddenly he slowed down and warned me that the path we were turning onto was steep and I needed to be watchful and careful. We turned off the high path and onto a transition path that would lead to the river. As we'd began our descent, we found it very rough and Dad had slowed down the pace to transition carefully. We needed to proceed slowly, or we could quickly tumble to the bottom. We had no other option; this was the only way to get to the river.

Quickly, the walk became difficult and challenging. Briar bushes hugged the path. I followed closely behind Dad as he'd instructed. When I started sliding, he'd been there to catch me. The path had loose dirt, and the slope was slippery. Not only was it slippery, but we had to look out for many obstacles: rocks, logs, holes, and so on. The high easy path was now behind us, but I did not have time to look back. Now we only had the time, energy, and strength to concentrate on each next step.

As Dad was leading, he would push the overgrown briar branches out of the way, and sometimes, when he released them, they would fly back and hit me right in the face. I felt like I needed more eyes. One eye to watch Dad, another eye to watch the branches, one to focus on the slippery slope, and another on the stuff I was carrying. Of course, I didn't have extra eyes to watch all those things, so I was glad Dad was there to help me. I was on high alert, not knowing what would happen next.

On the high path, I'd had a lot of time to run around, play and look about. I saw the rapidly moving river, the lush farms, and the playful little animals. None of this was possible traveling on the transition path. Instead, I'd been entirely focused on my next steps, keeping my balance, and not losing my footing. This path was quite the undertaking, but was the only way to get to the river below.

The transition road from the high path to the river may seem minor considering all the transitions happening throughout the world, but it had been a significant transition for me. When a transition is personal, it becomes substantial. The transition road was not long, but travelling on it could be very eventful. Things could go wrong quickly. I was happy once this path did what it was intended to do: transfer us from a place of ease and contemplation to a place of activity and adventure.

> God leads us
> through transitions
> to the places he
> wants us to go.

We transition from one task to another all the time. We transition from work to recreation, from cleaning the garage to washing the car, from doing the laundry to cooking a meal or from talking on the phone to working on the budget. These transitions occur almost unnoticed and can be called lateral transitions. They are overlooked and are the most common and least eventful transitions.

I believe God leads us through transitions to the places he wants us to go. When God leads, He will position us exactly where he wants us to be. God's positioning system (GPS) is at work. We should watch for it, and thank Him for it because he positions us in this way all the time.

Consistency in Ethics and Character

Every day I switch from my identity as the boss at work to a spouse at home; from attendance at a non-profit meeting to writing; or from being a friend to being a dad. During every transition, displaying consistency of ethical values and character is of paramount importance. My values, integrity, and beliefs need to be consistent throughout all facets of life, including transitions. I desire to always display inclusivity, generousity, kindness, humor, honesty, faithfulness, and many other character traits. It doesn't matter whether I am on the high path of contemplation, the path of transition, or the low path of activity—my character should remain the same.

When Dad and I began our transition, it was important for me to stay focused on what was coming up. Looking back could have caused me to take a tremendous fall, or caused me to get hit in the face by a branch or step into a hole. If I were to veer off course, I might even have ended up in a briar bush or tripping over a rock. I had to focus all of my energy on where I was going, not on where I'd been. We hadn't arrived yet.

Many scriptures speak to being in the moment. Living in the glory of yesterday will take away from today. God has planned something good for us, and we need to press on as the apostle, Paul, tells us:

13Brothers and sisters, I do not consider myself yet to have taken hold of it. But one thing I do: Forgetting what is behind and straining toward what is ahead, 14I press on toward the goal to win the prize for which God has called me heavenward in Christ Jesus. [Philippians 3:13-14]

Jesus tells us to not look back:

Jesus replied, No one who puts a hand to the plow and looks back is fit for service in the kingdom of God. [Luke 9:62]

If a never-changing God is doing a new thing in our lives, then we must not to be stagnant or live in the past. We must move forward. The prophet Isaiah encouraged us not to dwell on the past.

18Forget the former things; do not dwell on the past. 19See, I am doing a new thing! [Isaiah 43:18-19a]

The transition from the high path to the low path was not easy. We wanted to get to the river, so we had to transition. The high path would not have taken us to the river, but it did take us to a place of transition. We frequently do things that are necessary even though they may not be fun. Transition roads are often associated with pain and discomfort, but we must travel them.

Transitioning Up and Down

On a path of transition, down can be up and up can be down. Transitions can be up, down, or lateral. If a new job provides more power, more income, and better benefits, we say we are transitioning up. We usually desire this type of transition or move.

If we don't desire the move, we might say we are transitioning down. We would consider a new job with less power, a lower salary, and fewer benefits as transitioning down. We might even dread the thought of a down transition, but they are a part of life.

The transition at The Dead-End Road took us down to the river, but it was an up transition because it was one we desired. It took me to the place I had dreamed of going. When I transitioned from secular employment to full-time ministry, the transition was costly in prestige, salary, and benefits. From the world's viewpoint, it would be a down transition. Yet, because it was God-ordained and the desire of my heart, I considered it an up transition. After making the transition, I was no longer as popular, my pay was lower and I received less benefits. But God's guidance trumps all of these things. His benefits are eternal.

All God-ordained and orchestrated transitions are up transitions. If God is leading, who are we to get in the way? If God desires to move me and I don't want to move, it won't feel right to me until I go forward with it and maybe not even then. If God wants me to carry out a ministry in the inner city, but I would prefer to minister in a rural setting, doing what God wants will feel like a down transition at first, but in reality, it isn't. I must remember I cannot trust my feelings—I must trust God.

A few years ago, I visited Rick, a good friend of mine from the Detroit area. Rick gave me a guided tour of the Detroit area and a mini-tour of Michigan. During the tour while traveling on

Interstate Route 75 in Detroit, we went over a bridge. On both sides of the interstate, we saw dirty factories, run-down neighborhoods, and places that looked overcrowded and depressed. I whispered to God at that moment, "God, I will go anywhere, but please don't send me to the Detroit area." A couple of years later, He moved me to the Detroit downriver area. I know it was His will and I know He'd orchestrated that transition. In many ways it had felt like a down transition, but it wasn't. God knew what He was doing. I fell in love with the people and God used me wonderfully at that location. All transitions guided by God are up transitions.

No matter what happens, believers need to have trust and faith that God is in control. I have said, "Ouch, ouch, ouch," through many transitions in my life. But because an all-knowing, all-powerful, and ever-present God is leading me, I am glad for all the transitions that have brought me to this time in my life. It has been both exhilarating and opportunistic.

> **If God is leading, I need to trust and stay close to Him.**

I don't always like to transition and often hate the transition path but I know things will not change unless *I* change. On that trip as a boy, the transition path was the only way to the river; I could not catch fish unless I transitioned. The choices are clear: I can transition or stay on the same path. Those are my options. Even if I choose to remain on the same path, at some juncture, I will be *forced* to transition. If God is leading, I need to trust and stay close to Him—I need to follow Him—my Father.

Recently, I talked with a man that had been at the top of his organization. He'd been rewarded well because of his hard work and dedication. The pay was excellent and the benefits adequate and he liked his job. The downside was that this job was extremely stressful and limited the amount of time he could spend with his family.

The governing board of this organization experienced a complete change of directors, and they unanimously decided to go a new and different direction. They called my friend into a lonely office and released him. They desired a younger person who was more liberal and modernistic. My friend was taken back by their decision because he had worked very hard and put in all the hours necessary to do superior work and was very good at his job. He was well-liked by both employees and constituents, yet now he was unemployed.

When the Board Director had let him go, he'd been in complete shock. Many thoughts had gone through his head. Thoughts of failure; thoughts asking *How dare they?* and *How can I support my family?* He described to me how as he'd packed his things, he'd been packing up countless memories.

When he'd gotten into his car to go home that afternoon, he said he'd had a supernatural release of a heavy load. A burden had lifted from his shoulders. He hadn't realized how much stress he *had* been carrying. Strangely, he felt good about it. His transition would take him from a very active low path to a much needed slower-paced high path. He desperately needed it. After he'd been on the high path for a while, positive things happened. Family time increased significantly. He made several positive adjustments to his lifestyle. Eventually, he was ready to transition again and was soon offered a position with another firm. The new job involved less stress and he had every weekend off. Not only were the benefits better, but he also earned more income than at his previous job. He would have never chosen this path, but in looking back, he saw how God had been taking care of him.

At times, stepping onto the transition path may seem very chaotic and dangerous. On that first fishing excursion, the transition to the river was terrifying. I feared I would slip and fall into the river. I feared I would be injured, which would result in pain. I didn't want to experience any of those things. Sudden transitions from the high path are very similar.

Transitions from the low path to the high path are different. On the low path of action, you'll find great activity and constant challenge. It is easy to get stressed out on the low path due to endless responsibilities and nagging pressures. When my plate is full and I become fearful that I cannot handle one more thing, it's time for me to seek transition to the high path to contemplate things in depth. When I step onto the path of transition, I feel immediate relief. Transitioning away from the stressors of the low path makes me thankful for the relief.

Discussion Questions

1. Do you remember a time in your life when things seemed to be going very smoothly almost to the point of boredom then all of sudden you found yourself on a path of transition? If so, describe the actual process of transition. Was it scary? Was it risky?
2. Have you ever transitioned into a very chaotic situation? What obstacles did you face? Did you feel like you were on a slippery slope?
3. Dad was there for me on that first fishing trip when we transitioned from the high road to the river. I was unable to physically see everything that could have been dangerous and was glad Dad was there. Likewise today, God is always with me. Have you ever felt His presence while you were transitioning? Have you ever not felt his presence during a transition?

4. Have you ever looked back and understood how God had been with you during a transition, even though you'd wondered where he was at the time of the transition?
5. Have you ever been so busy and stressed that you felt immediate relief once you stepped onto the path of transition?
6. Are you or someone you know on the path of transition right now? If so, describe it.

Prayer

My Lord and my God, I thank you for your presence. I always ask for your guidance, and you've often led me onto the path of transition. Sometimes I struggle with that, but you know best. I know that all things work together for good for those who are saved and called according to Your purpose. Forgive me when I fear and fight the transition. Forgive me when I become too comfortable and fail to do what You have called me to do. Continue to use me, Father. Keep leading me along whatever path you desire me to travel. I desperately need you. Thank you for being my God, Lord, and Savior, and also my guide. I pray this in the precious name of Jesus. Amen.

Launch Team Comments

One thing came to mind when thinking about walking along that slippery slope: I remember always looking for a rock, tree root, or something solid on which I could put my foot. I suppose we all have needed to be alert and looking out for those timely, well-positioned landing places on our journey. God provides those for us. Our job is to be looking for them. B.E.

I wanted to leave my job. It was draining and frustrating and weighed on me more and more with each day. I had the support of my wife to do so, but as the responsibility and accountability grew, I didn't think I could. Finally, it overwhelmed me, when my employer decided to fire three people and give me all their work. This forced me to leave my comfort zone of a well-paying job and do what I've always wanted to. A.O.

I have been on the path of transition for a while. I've made many decisions that have brought a lot of change in my life and was very stressed for a while. I realize that huge amounts of stress will take away our peace. I have let go of the stress and am on the high road to peace of mind. I have had to manage my time well to accomplish all that I need to do in a day. Sometimes life can be very overwhelming. I try to remember to take it one day at a time and when needed, get to the high path. M.F.

When we were preparing to move from Florida to Michigan, I wasn't sure I wanted to live in Michigan. I am not someone who likes change, and am not fond of very cold weather. I was in my late forties, and I thought, who wants to hire anyone my age? And besides, I didn't know anyone in Michigan. God showed me this was where He wanted me to be, and I grew to love Taylor, Michigan and the church. The people in the Taylor church and community became some of my dearest friends. D.W.F.

When it comes to transitions—even those seemingly forced upon us—we still have one huge personal choice to make, and that is to pray. I've experienced two very difficult transitions during my years of pastoring. The first was made difficult by me as I resisted the Lord's leading, by refusing to move when he wanted me to move. During that time, I struggled with the situation, with my ministry, with my family, with myself and with God. The other transition, while difficult emotionally, was not nearly as painful because I stayed in communication with God and trusted Him. I didn't understand the whys and wherefores, but I had God's peace as I cooperated with Him during the transition. C.W.

As I reflect on transitions, I think of many that I have experienced in my life. Some were agreeable and I'd looked forward to them, while others were unpleasant and not of my choosing. My ability as a Christian to reflect and look back at what happened as a result of transition (good or bad) has strengthened my trust in God. Although Romans 8:28 is an often misused verse and taken out of context, I can't help but bring it to mind. I am who and what I am today because God has worked for my good even in transitions that were unpleasant for me at the time. Being forced to cut a snagged line and losing a favorite fishing lure may have been unpleasant at the time, but maybe it could have been that unhealthy lure you talk about in a later chapter. That is a transition I wouldn't have chosen for myself, but God in His infinite mercy provided something much better. Trust in God has been proven for me in my life. Illustrations and stories about surviving the storms of life, when viewed from a spiritual perspective, reflect our Father's perfect love for us. R.E.

Chapter Four

The Low Path of Action

My favorite path is the path of action. At the Dead-End Road, the path of action was the low path, where we caught fish. It was, by far, the most exciting path and in the middle of all the action. Everything moved quickly, and this was where I desired to be. The path of action appears to be the most fruitful of the three paths. There's no time to be bored as it's cutting edge and fast-paced. Welcome to the path of action, where there are decisions to be made, work to be done, and adventure to explore.

> *14What good is it, my brothers and sisters, if someone claims to have faith but has no deeds? Can such faith save them? 15Suppose a brother or a sister is without clothes and daily food. 16If one of you says to them, Go in peace; keep warm and well fed, but does nothing about their physical needs, what good is it? 17In the same way, faith by itself, if it is not accompanied by action, is dead. [James 2:14-17]*

In the Center of Adventure

The path of transition had a steep slope, and we took it slowly all the way. We used different muscles on the transition path because of how steep it was. Had we not put on the brakes while transitioning, we could have fallen on our faces or into the Olentangy River. That would not have been a pretty sight. So we held back the momentum that was pulling us downward toward the low path of action. Abruptly, the slope on the transition path flattened out, and thankfully the tension in our legs could be released. I can't imagine walking like that for a long distance.

When we arrived at the low path, we instinctively slowed down to a pace that required us to put new effort into our walking. Although we hadn't arrived at the place where we would actually fish, Dad said that we were not far away from it. He was looking for a safe area where we could set up our chairs, have room to cast our lines, and where I would not get into too much mischief.

I had been dreaming about this place. Those moments at my first fishing spot with Dad were exciting to me. As the adventure began to unfold, I was full of energy and anticipation. Many years later, the memory of that day's activities have become very precious to me. Finally, I had arrived at the place where Dad would teach me to fish. In good time, he would show me all I needed to know about catching fish.

The low path was much different than the contemplative high path. It was also different than the rapidly descending path of transition. On the low path of action, we traveled very close to the river. The path didn't have any guard rails to keep me from falling in the river, and there were all sorts of obstacles along the way. I knew that soon we would be fishing in the Olentangy River.

I wasn't sure what to do and I didn't know how to do much of anything, but I knew Dad would patiently teach me. I had traveled where my heart has always wanted to be—in the center of the action. I was at the place where a dream became reality: the dream of catching fish with Dad; and it was the priority that day.

We were on the action path, where the action was unpredictable and where Dad began to teach me how to fish, about manhood and about living an adventuous life. He taught me the fundamentals of fishing and life principles that I use every day. After experiencing this place, it was where I desired to be. Activity was all around us. I wanted to forever be on the action path where all the adventure, action, and fun was happening.

Sights and Sounds

I learned to listen and found it to be an exciting exercise. I tried to hear the things Dad began to point out to me. Learning to identify one noise among many noises seemed to be an art that my dad had perfected. On the path of action, there was no boredom as the sounds of activity surrounded me. Dad taught me that each sound had a source.

I also began to notice how phenomenal the sights were close to the water and on the land around us. The activity of the river was awesome. I was close enough to see the little fish swimming in and out of the weeds. Were they baby fish? I had no idea, but I thought they must be babies until I drew closer and saw a real baby fish. A snake slithered by with its head above the water. Suddenly, I heard something and followed the sound to a big grandpa bullfrog. I decided he must have been a grandpa because he had a low voice.

I wanted to stop and watch the fish, but we were on a mission to find a fishing spot. I wanted to throw something at the bullfrog, but dad told me to leave him alone, so I did. The snake was scary to me, and I was immediately more cautious.

Butterflies, dragonflies, horseflies, and several other insects flew through the air. I discovered some blackened, charred logs from a burnt-out fire. Dad taught me how to make a flat stone bounce across the water. I had given no thought to any of this when Dad had invited me to go fishing. But now it was a reality, and I saw all those extras as a blessing from Dad.

When we'd arrived at the spot where we would fish, we set down our fishing poles and equipment. Dad unfolded the chairs. I was very excited about fishing, but I also loved *all* the extra Dad blessings: rocks, fallen trees, fast-moving water, blue sky, and sounds that I had never heard before. I saw fish that would jump out of the water, and I imagined they were trying to get my attention because they were hungry. Mysterious bubbles would come up from the bottom of the river. I'd wondered if a fish had caused those bubbles? Something had to cause them. Seeing an owl swoop down below the tree branches with its wide wingspan was thrilling. I hadn't known that birds that big existed.

The sounds were terrific near the river. One bird sounded like it was saying, "Bob White." I found this especially funny because we knew a man named Bob White. Whip-poor-wills were whip-poor-willing, while the squirrels jumped from limb to limb far above our heads. I found out that ducks really do quack and geese often honk. The path of action at the river offered a real education. The wind-blown leaves in the trees reminded me of many hands applauding the creation that I was experiencing. White fluffy clouds reminded me of balls of cotton as they moved across the blue sky. Various things floated on the river from upstream to downstream: a leaf, a dead fish, a candy wrapper, an empty can, a runaway bobber, and more. Watching and being in the middle of all the action was a lot of fun—where my little-boy energy met great opportunity.

Enjoying the Moment

I wanted to watch the fish swim around the shoreline. I wanted to throw something at the grandpa bullfrog. I wanted to watch the water where the fish had jumped to see if it would jump again. I wanted to watch that snake and see where he went. Starting way back then, I wanted to stop and enjoy the moment just a little bit longer. This desire remains today—the desire to savor the coffee, to smell the roses and to stay in the moment. But doing so is not always feasible. Life moves on at a phenomenal speed, especially on the path of action, and I must move on, too.

From the time I was little, I've felt that I was on a mission and that I needed to enjoy the lifelong journey that I am on. It won't stop, even if we decide to. Many of the moments God has given us are like Dad blessings, only they are *God* blessings: little extras attached to our mission and purpose in life.

Sounds are a symphony playing in the background of life. I think God wants me to trace the sounds back to their source, the way Dad taught me. It takes time, but finding the source is like receiving a bonus from God. I have developed this skill over time. Even when many voices are all around, I often trace a single voice back to its source; maybe to a child that might be trying to get my attention.

Many birds may be singing their special song but I often trace the sound to a single bird. Possibly a dove sitting on the fence outside my home. When I've heard the whip-poor-will, bobwhite and others, I've tried to trace their songs to the originator of the sound. Identifying the source always becomes an added blessing. It's not always easy, but it's always worthwhile, and becomes a blessed accomplishment.

> Sounds are a symphony playing in the background of life.

Being with Dad on that first fishing trip sixty-five years ago was special for him, and memorable for me. Dad taught me things that I've used, thought about often, and continue to dwell upon to this very day. Being with Dad that day was certainly a blessing that lasted only a brief moment in all of eternity. This God-given moment was significant—a gift orchestrated by God and given to me. I hadn't done anything to deserve this gift.

Life is full of God-given moments. For much of my life, I didn't understand they were from God. But, I do now. My Dad and I were at the river on a very active path, and our Father God had orchestrated it all.

Discussion Questions

1. We have discussed the high path of contemplation, the middle path of transition, and the low path of action. Think about and discuss a time in your life when you've experienced these paths. Think about various scenarios in life: a new home, job loss, increase in income, death of a loved one, personal pain, moving out of state, the first day of school, etc. Try to determine what path you think you were on when these events occured.
2. Do you experience and recognize God's bonuses as blessings? When was the last time you experienced a God bonus or a God moment?
3. Go for a short walk and listen to the symphony of sounds around you. Try to locate the source of these sounds. Look around and do not stop walking until you recognize a God bonus.
4. Take some time today for God moments. They may be in silence. They may be in the middle of action. They may occur in the noisiest of places. Try to experience God's bonuses, and God moments every day, and thank Him for them.

Prayer

Thank you, Father, for this day. Forgive me for missing the God bonuses that you have given to me. I often take them for granted because you generously pour your blessings on me. Thank you for those you have put around me and for the God moments, I have enjoyed them. Lord, lead me to more God bonuses and God moments and Holy Spirit, and please make me aware of these very special times. God, I know that you are with me always and that my entire life is a God moment—help me walk knowing that truth. Thank you for the path of action and for allowing me to experience the adventure of life with you. Help me to be a blessing and a God bonus in someone today. I pray this in Jesus's name, Amen.

Launch Team Comments

I feel I've been through this and continue to go through it. Leaving my job and taking the risk to start my own business has been hugely stressful and challenging. It's had its faults, but was the best thing I'd ever done for my career. Some days I feel I can't do anymore, and others, that I can't do enough. But I keep at it every day and trust that what I am doing is what I am supposed to do. A.O.

The Path of Action is a challenging path—whispers of failure spoken to a heart that desires perfection and lacks the confidence in the source of her value changes a door to a window. I can see the path but feel safe to just look. A gentle hand on my back, helping me move forward are the words of encouragement spoken from a friend. These remind me that I am not enough, but the resources of a loving God will bring the provision I need. I may resist His plan and His pace, but only until the revelation comes that His best is His plan for me and this story He has written for me can be filled by no other. D.W.

Chapter Five

Don't Let Your Hook Show

When I go fishing, I use many types and sizes of hooks. Hooks are sharp, and they hurt if they penetrate the skin. I didn't like playing around with them because I'd often get hooked, and I know first hand, hooks hurt.

Likewise, when I allow my anger, bad attitude, or any number of negative emotions and personality quirks to show, I am allowing my figurative hook to show. Much like when an angry bear shows its claws and teeth, when someone allows their hooks to show, it negatively effects relationships. These hooks can damage and be very destructive. I'm always sorry when I realize my hooks have been showing. I need God to help me recognize my hooks and to be aware of how they affect others.

8Finally, all of you, be like-minded, be sympathetic, love one another, be compassionate and humble. 9Do not repay evil with evil or insult with insult. On the contrary, repay evil with blessing, because to this you were called so that you may inherit a blessing. 10For, "Whoever would love life and see good days must keep their tongue from evil and their lips from deceitful speech. 11They must turn from evil and do good; they must seek peace and pursue it. 12For the eyes of the Lord are on the righteous, and his ears are attentive to their prayer, but the face of the Lord is against those who do evil." [1 Peter 3:8-12]

Treacherous Hooks

I will always be grateful to Dad for teaching me about fishing. He taught me all about hooks and how I had to be careful with them. He also taught me to cast the line. Learning how to cast without getting the hook stuck in a bush, or a tree, or my clothing was very tricky. After many, many attempts, I finally got the hang of it. But hooks can be treacherous.

Starting with that first fishing trip, Dad almost always caught the first fish. I'd been taught to be happy when good things happened to other people, so I was okay with Dad catching the first fish—elated even—because I just knew that I would catch the next fish. One time, after he caught the first one, Dad caught another fish, and another, and then another. I hadn't gotten even a nibble on my line. I was no longer happy for him. I was full-blown jealous. I may have even yelled out, "This isn't fair!" or "Don't you get it, God? Dad is catching fish, and I'm not."

Dad had been watching me, and I am sure he saw my attitude change. He'd suggested that I place my line closer to his. Maybe there was a school of fish right below where he was fishing. I'd been eager to do that and hoping he would suggest it. The result, however, was the same—he continued to catch fish, but I didn't. Next, he suggested that I check my bait. I pulled my line in and saw the worm. So I thought the bait was fine. "Looks okay to me," I said sarcastically.

He then asked if the hook was showing. What did he mean by that? I looked at my bait a little closer. Sure enough, the worm had wiggled its way off part of the hook. That shiny pointed hook was visible. If I were a fish, I wouldn't bite that worm either. I pushed that Houdini worm back on the hook and cast it back in the water. The next thing I knew, the fish were biting, and I caught a fish. Checking to see whether the hook is showing has become routine for me whenever I go fishing. One of the little secrets to fishing is knowing that the fish won't bite if they can see the hook.

Avoiding Hooks

As a pastor, I cannot think of a single person that I do not sincerely love. I desire the very best for everyone I know. I want them to be saved and know Jesus, live a full and abundant life, and go to heaven. My desire is for them to be happy and have hope, peace, joy, love, faith, and more. All of the things I want for myself—I hope they receive as well.

The truth is, I might not be the very best thing for a lot of people. Some people wear on my nerves, and I'm sure I wear on some people's nerves, too. I'd help them, but I don't necessarily want to hang out with them. If certain people don't come to my dinner table tonight, I will not be disappointed. My love for them does not rely on having a best-friend relationship with them. It might be best if we stay away from each other. Some relationships and personalities mix like oil and water—not very well. My love for all people is sincere. I desire the best for them and, in some cases, I know that I am not part of that.

Some types of people, even though I love them, are tough for me to be around. Things they do, their mannerisms, or things they say make me anxious. They have hooks that are visible to me. Hooks—such as personality quirks and preferences—are displayed through temperament and emotions, and we all have them. Some of these hooks bother me but might not bother you or they may bother you and might not bother me.

I find it difficult, for example, to be around people who are extremely loud and obnoxious. It's not that I don't love them. Quite to the contrary! At a football game, my wife, Dottie, usually gets extremely loud and obnoxious. A friend of ours also gets loud and obnoxious, just like her. When our friend is also at the same game, they often sit together, and I often sit a couple of rows behind my obnoxious friend and loud, boisterous, whistling wife. I sit beside my friend's wife and he sits with mine and this has become somewhat of a joke. I don't associate well with loud and obnoxious people—not even my wife of forty-eight years. I'm just glad she and our friend are not that way all the time.

Avoiding hooks can be a two-way street. Dottie would rather not sit beside me at a game because she resents me telling her not to yell, scream, whistle, or be obnoxious. She likes doing those things when she is supporting her team. I get it! We both enjoy the game, but we enjoy it better if we do not sit next to each other. She can yell, scream, and be obnoxious, and we don't have to feel uncomfortable being next to each other.

I am a very organized person. I like to plot our trips: where we will take breaks, where we will eat, where we will spend the night, how many miles we will travel in a day, etc. I often make checklists and work hard to check off everything on the list. My wife liked that about me early in our marriage, but not so much anymore. She gets a little annoyed with me trying to schedule every minute of our vacation. She likes spontinaity, so we compromise and I limit my scheduling.

When we were first married, Dottie was extremely quiet, and I liked that about her while we were dating because of the mystery it created. I never knew for sure what she was thinking. Then after we'd been married for a time, it upset me a little bit that she was so quiet, and that I never knew what she was thinking. Since those early years, she now talks and shares her feelings much more—I think you get the picture. We all have personality quirks and habits that others may not appreciate. Those quirks and habits are like visible hooks.

In today's "gotta be me" society, we often forget to extend the courtesy of treating others the way they would like to be treated. Often, carefully refraining from intentionally repulsing someone by what we say or how we act can be an easy task of awareness. If we're aware that one of our personality quirks bothers someone else, we can act differently and hide that hook. We can decide to be sensitive to others's desires and wishes. For example, people who incessantly curse rarely do that around me, because I'm a minister. I often observe them carefully choosing their words. It is almost comical—they are hiding their hook. Our personality and individual preferences contain hooks that cause some people to run from us. Anyone observing these hooks can find humor in them, but they do turn people away from us. We need to be aware of them or we lose opportunities to make friends and deepen relationships (catching fish). Jesus alluded to this:

> *"Come, follow me," Jesus said, "and I will send you out to fish for people." [Mark 1:17]*

Revealing Our Hooks

It would be fair to say we all let our hooks show at times. I know I do. With awareness and effort, we do have some control over them. We may try very hard, for example, not to allow our hooks to show when we are around people we are trying to impress professionally or

> We all let our hooks show at times.

socially. We watch our emotions and display our best character traits to project a positive image. Sometimes we succeed, and sometimes we fail.

Unfortunately, when we go home to the people we love the most, our hooks usually show. The people that are closest to us are the most likely to experience the hurt and sting of our emotion-driven hooks. Outsiders would run, but those closest to us have little choice except to tolerate our sharp edges and verbal attacks.

In hindsight, we may realize that our hook was showing and discern that we've hurt those we love. We may feel bad and apologize, but the hook has already made its mark. Our apology sounds lame, even to us. We then try to make up for our loose tongue, anger, bad attitude, sarcasm, or unwarranted outbursts, but we can only do damage repair; we cannot roll back the clock and make it disappear.

We are more prone to allowing our emotion-driven hooks to be seen when we are tired, weak and vulnerable. Following is a list of situations that have caused me to reveal my hooks. My hooks show most often when:

- I've had a very stressful day
- I did not get enough sleep
- I have a huge to-do list
- I am extremely hungry
- Someone has failed to do something I've asked them to do
- I am disappointed
- I have failed at something and am disappointed with myself
- I am hurt or grieving
- I am depressed
- I'm angry at something or someone

Character Traits and Flaws

To identify and properly manage some of our emotional hooks may require the help of a professional therapist. Our thinking sometimes loses reason and becomes an illness that negatively effects life function. Three of these emotional issues are chronic bitterness, ongoing grief, and persistent pessimism.

CHRONIC BITTERNESS is often caused by something in life that scars us. Bitterness is not attractive; even when we believe it is warranted, it is repulsive. People do not like being around a bitter person. Bitterness can quickly become an emotion-driven hook. An angry and bitter person may need the help of a therapist to begin healing the emotional scars. Abused and bullied people often suppress their feelings, and build fences of isolation. These fences are impossible to penetrate. Isolated and bitter people seldom live happy, full, and abundant lives. Sometimes a pastor or a therapist can help get to the root causes of their bitterness and rescue them from a miserable existance so they can enjoy life. God knows the source of all bitterness and He understands how each person feels. He hears the cries of each person and is always available to rescue those perishing with bitterness. Turning to Him and confessing our bitterness are the first steps to healing.

ONGOING GRIEF can be brought on by the death of a loved one, the ending of a relationship, or the loss of something cherished. Some people are able to deal with grief and get on with their lives while others become stuck in grief. Grief duration is often connected to the severity of the loss. Chronic grievers have described their grief as something they cannot get over. They describe it as a long, dark tunnel or a deep, inescapeable pit. Ongoing grief is often accompanied by

> To identify and properly manage some of our emotional hooks may require the help of a professional therapist.

deep depression and exhaustion. Some become angry, while others decide to isolate themselves. The Bible instructs us to weep with those who weep, but how long should we continue to weep with those who weep continually? Grief counseling is often needed and is available at churches, funeral homes and therapist offices. A very kind and patient good friend can also be a huge help with recovering from grief. An effective counselor helps the grieving person identify the good times and to relive them by remembering. Successfully moving out of the pit of grief and depression will help the grieving person make new memories. When this happens, a breakthough often occurs and grief's grip is loosened. One reason God has given us our memory is to allow our joys in life to be replayed.

PERSISTENT PESSIMISM is a hook that most people try to stay away from. Many people are lonely because they are almost always negative, thinking the worst, and unable to articulate or identify the good in people, places, or things. Their pessimism keeps them from enjoying the good things of life. They think about what could go wrong instead of what could go right. Even when things are excellent or praiseworthy, they find something negative to say. This is a real turn off (a hook) to people enjoying life. Pessimistic people describe good things followed by the conjunction *but*. They usually start by describing something as "great, but..." then they continue with negative talk... negative talk... negative talk. The conjunction in this case is between two opposites: something extremely good and something extremely bad. Negativism is a hook that causes others to run from us. A friend can help change this behavior by lovingly pointing it out. A professional therapist, the church, a pastor or a small group can also help. Pessimistic people are living in the basement of life and they often appear determined to bring others down to the basement as well. Pastors, small groups, therapists, and others are available to help the persistant pessimist move toward a hopeful optimistic future.

We could spend time discussing problematic character traits and flaws, such as a contentious attitude, cursing, erratic emotions, negative thinking, apathy, indifference, arrogance, laziness, apprehension, aggression, being over-reactive, uncaring, pushy, lethargic, hypocritical, a know-it-all, etc. We know that a person who chronically displays any of these traits—hooks—will find people distancing themselves from them.

In fact, we all have character traits, emotions, and flaws that make people feel uncomfortable. These traits are not appealing. Some of my character traits, such as overanalyzing, extreme introversion, and oversimplification of life, push people away from me. Ironically, while these push some people away, they often draw other people *toward* me. Despite these traits, it's important to give people the benefit of the doubt, overlook their weaknesses, find their strengths, and get to know who they are.

At the fishing spot, the fish wouldn't bite when the hook was visible because the worm had partially wiggled its way to freedom. Strangely enough, fish *will* bite an artificial lure on a hook that is visible. I've heard that in those cases, some fish bite because of the movement of the lure, the flash of reflective light on the lure, or as a way to fight off the lure as it passes through the water. The key to fishing is to become familiar with the hook, the lure, or bait that works, and the fish. Likewise, the key to life is to understand yourself, know people, and treat everyone as they would like to be treated. We can only do that with God's help.

Discussion Questions

1. Do you have a hook that you are you aware of that has caused people to distance themselves from you? Some valuable traits—for example, devout in following Christ—can distance people from you as well. What can you do?
2. Why do you think we are the last to know when our hook is visible in a relationship? How can we become more cognizant of how others are responding to us?
3. Without naming the person, is there someone in your life that you would cross the street to avoid? Why do you respond to them that way?

4. Why do you think we reveal our hooks to those closest to us that we love the most? What can we do to be less confrontational with family and those we love?
5. Are any of your relationships strained because of your hooks? Because of their hooks? Spend time with God and ask Him to help you understand how to deal with them better.

Prayer

Father, you have made me unique and wonderful. You help me edify the body of Christ, the church. I desire to be a blessing and to draw people to you. I often fail to portray hope and peace and love the way you would like me to. Help me to become more like Jesus. Help me to be an attractive witness about your marvelous hope. Guide me to control my tongue and to use my voice to glorify you. Help me to recognize when I'm not doing so and when I am hurting others. I love you, Lord, and pray this in the precious, powerful name of Jesus. Amen.

Launch Team Comments

I would say I show my hook more to the people I love the most! Sadly, I will move heaven and earth to hide my hook at work or with my friends. I become exhausted, trying to be what others need. Then, I return home—to the people I would give my life for—depleted, frustrated, exhausted, and raw! My hook is very visible, at times. Ashamed, I must admit that it is fully exposed. I am working on saying "No" to more commitments, so I have the mental and emotional stamina to serve my family with the same joy and fullness I strive for elsewhere. L.F.H.

I can approach people whose hooks are showing. It's easier if I'm actively ministering. But in my replenishment time, I am not able to go there as easily! Sometimes I rely on God to fill me with compassion but other times I withdraw. I try to notice when my nonverbals are unattractive, but sometimes I can't seem to help it. I often need community support! C.M.H.

I did not grow up in a Christian home and did not know Jesus Christ as Savior or how I could grow in His love. From childhood to early adulthood, it seemed many people bullied me. The bullies caused me to be angry and bitter. Then Jesus came into my life, and many things changed, mostly me. I used to allow my hook to show because of the hurt that I was feeling. As a result, I lashed out and hurt other people. I learned to control this much better, and the Lord has made the difference. D.W.F.

Chapter Six

Sincere Trust

Trust is gained over time but it can be destroyed in a moment. Trust can be earned, learned, and sometimes burned. Trusting God, ourselves, and others is—at best—a delicate mix of total trust, cautious trust, and distrust. The inability to trust is the reason why people build impenetrable walls, where truthfulness cannot be shared. Walls do two things. They limit our freedom and keep people out of our lives. Unfortunately, these walls are everywhere. I pray that walls never exists in our relationship with God or with those we love the most. May we always grow and learn to trust our relationship with God, others, and ourselves.

> Trust is gained over time but it can be destroyed in a moment.

5Trust in the LORD with all your heart and lean not on your own understanding; 6in all your ways submit to him, and he will make your paths straight. [Proverbs 3:5-6]

May the God of hope fill you with all joy and peace as you trust in him, so that you may overflow with hope by the power of the Holy Spirit. [Romans 15:13]

Trusting Dad

From the very early planning stages of the fishing trip, I listened and trusted Dad. It didn't just begin with the fishing trip; from my earliest recollection, I have been able to trust Dad. Dad would often tell me to trust him, and I did. He'd never given me any reason not to. I knew him as a man who kept his promise; he'd promised to take me fishing and there we were. That promise was one I could trust from a man that I loved at a time when I needed him. I trusted Dad, and as I learned more about the trip, my trust grew stronger. I trusted that I'd have an exciting time gathering nightcrawlers the night before. I trusted that I'd have my fishing pole and that Dad and I would have a packed lunch and snacks prepared by Mom. I had a confident trust and a faith that these things would happen—and they did, just as Dad had planned and promised.

When we'd arrived at the Dead-End Road and found that barrier across it, my heart sank for a moment. But I trusted Dad. He parked the car and we began our journey on the paths toward the Olentangy River. One of the best things I ever did was trust Dad.

We came across some huge obstacles as we walked the paths of the river: a series of muddy puddles that needed careful navigation, a fallen tree that we needed to climb over, a slippery rock that we stepped across, and more. It was treacherous at times. I was sometimes afraid of getting hurt and not being able to conquer the challenges. Dad encouraged me and helped me the best he could. Even when I feared an obstacle, I trusted Dad and moved forward.

Still afraid, I began to move over and around obstacles. I listened carefully to Dad as he talked me through each challenge, and I trusted

> My courage was never the result of any lack of fear but of continuing in spite of it.

what he was telling me to do. I proved my trust by being obedient and carefully following his instructions. Sometimes I failed and sometimes I succeeded; yet I always tried. My courage was never the result of any lack of fear but of continuing in spite of it.

Trusting Myself

We needed to carry a lot of equipment and supplies to the place where we would fish. Dad loaded me up, and then carried the rest of the equipment. The load seemed large, and I was afraid I couldn't carry it. I was uncomfortable and found it difficult to walk holding the burden. But Dad had more confidence in me than I had in myself. After all, he was the one that had loaded me up. I needed to learn to trust in my abilities. I knew Dad wouldn't put anything on me that I could not handle.

Each path that we navigated as we walked toward the river presented unique challenges. Dad walked faster than me on the easy high path which made it a challenge to walk faster with a heavy load. The path of transition was steep and slippery. I dropped stuff along the way, but picked it back up and kept moving. On the path of action, my load seemed heavier as it brushed against the bushes and I ducked under low-hanging branches and climbed over or went around every imaginable obstacle. Walking each path was a test of different abilities.

Developing trust appeared to demand proof. Not until my abilities were tested and proven could I begin to trust them fully. Without testing, I would never have known what I could accomplish. I fell many times, but I got back up, brushed myself off, and kept going. Through these trials and tests, I learned to trust in myself and my abilities.

When we'd made it to the river and to the fishing spot, Dad began to teach me. I'd had so much to learn: how to bait my hook, how to cast, how to change bobber depth, how to recognize when a fish was biting, how to stand, things to watch out for, how to recognize poison weeds, how to set the hook, how to turn on the clicker, how to adjust the drag, etc. After beginning to fish, he told me to reel in a short distance to tighten the slack in my line. Too much slack made it impossible to successfully set the hook if a fish would bite. If I reeled in my line enough to get rid of the slack, then I would be too close to the shore, and would have to cast out my line again. Dad warned me about getting hung up on the low branches, weeds, and rocks in the river. He taught me new skills at a phenomenal rate, and I had so much to learn. I knew I wasn't retaining all of it, and I was concerned that maybe I would never get it. He had already shared so much and I had much more knowledge to learn. Would I ever be able to trust the knowledge I had?

I began to learn that I could trust myself. My abilities proved to be adequate; I made mistakes at first, but things began to come together. As time went on and my experience grew, I became better at fishing. As Dad continued teaching me, I became good at many of the things he taught me. My developing abilities gave me confidence, and with confidence, I learned to trust in those abilities. I became capable of many skills and was anxious to learn and try new skills. I grew to understand that my capabilities were more extensive than I'd thought. Trusting Dad, myself, my abilities, and my knowledge was a large part of the success I realized at the Dead-End Road and throughout life.

Trusting Others

As time went on, we invited others to fish with us. My mom, brothers, uncles, cousins, and an occasional friend went with us and I soon had a number of teachers. They added to what Dad had already taught me, including little tricks about fishing they had discovered. Uncle Bob taught Dad and me the fisherman's knot, as he called it. He used it to tie hooks, swivels and lures onto his fishing line. His knot held better and was faster to tie than the multiple granny knots that we'd been using. After we'd mastered the fisherman's knot, we used it from that day forward. I still use it today. Listening to the instruction and advice of other people resulted in becoming a better fisherman. I learned to trust others, but also learned I needed to *test* their instructions.

Admittedly, I was gullible to a fault; most five-year-old boys are. And my brothers were often pranksters. Quite often, I became the brunt of their jokes. To my misfortune, I believed what they told me, and trusted them way too often. One day, they told me that if I'd step on a floating log in the river, it would hold me up and would be fun. The log was tiny, only about three feet long, with a diameter of just a few inches.

I hesitantly stepped on the log, but when I transferred my weight to the log, it sank to the bottom. My shoe, foot, sock, and trouser leg followed the log to the bottom of the river. Everything, including my feelings, was soaked. I'd believed them, and now they were laughing at my gullibility and mishap. The wet leg and foot didn't bother me as much as their laughter. Their humor at my expense stung a little. At five years old, I knew better than to talk to strangers, but they did not come any stranger than my brothers.

I *can* thank my brothers for teaching me that I should be cautious when trusting others.

Trusting God

Fast forward one year when I was six. I met Gary, my best friend, in first grade when my family moved into our first brand new home. Funny how that very small house seemed so spacious. Gary lived on the corner lot and our side yard connected to his backyard. We wore a path in the grass from our side door to his rear garage door.

We did everything together and enjoyed the same things. Our clubhouse was under his basement steps. A large blanket was stapled to the stairs, giving us a curtain of privacy. Gary had run an extension cord to and placed a light in our clubhouse. It was just a naked bulb hanging from one of the stairs above us, but it was very cool to meet and play in our little part of the basement. We had records and a record player in the clubhouse. We would often buy a quart of pop and some chips and take it into our clubhouse. We liked to dip our chips in the pop filling up those air bubbles that many of the chips had, and then we would eat them. The pop was often room temperature, but we thought it was cool playing records, drinking pop, eating chips and plotting and planning where our friendship would take us next.

We rode our little bikes, walked in the woods, fished in the creek, and hiked in the fields. Why, we even took off all our clothes and ran naked in the cornfield. It was our way of pretending we were living in the jungle or wilderness where they had no clothes. Nobody knew—not even Mom! Just Gary and I.

In the fifth grade, my family moved thirty-five miles away. Gary and I continued to be best friends. Throughout the summer, he stayed at my house for a couple of weeks, and then I would stay at his house. It was great to be with him as I missed all of our adventures. Until the move, we had been inseparable.

Sadly, I was learning that all earthly roads come to an end. A year later, when I was in the sixth grade, something happened that I will always remember. My parents picked me up at school—something they'd never done before. I knew something was up. They broke the news to me that Gary had drowned in a farm pond. A group of boys from my old neighborhood had decided to get on a raft that was by the farmer's pond. They'd pushed the raft into the deep area, and it had capsized. Two of the boys couldn't swim: Gary and another friend of mine. They both drowned. I wept the entire night and then became very depressed. The depression lingered, and although I had met many other kids at my new school, I wasn't as close to any of them as I had been to Gary.

The year was 1961, and that summer I had been invited to the Richland County Fair for a week with one of the 4-H guys I had met. His name was Eddie, and he had two ponies. I enjoyed riding his ponies, and Eddie seemed like a good boy, so my parents told me I should go. They'd thought that it might help me with my depression. They even gave me twenty dollars to spend. I was glad the meals were free because Eddie and I spent the entire twenty dollars on the first day. We played games, rode rides, and ate a ton of junk food.

On day two of the fair, my depression was extremely heavy. I walked alone around the fairgrounds. The background noise was loud, the lights on the rides were flashing, and the games were colorful and inviting, but they all cost money. Eddie was busy showing his prized ponies and hanging out with his 4-H friends. I felt all alone as I walked through the fairgrounds thinking, *Without money, there is nothing to do. God, why did I ever come here?*

I did not expect an answer to that question, but immediately, something remarkable happened. A man, whom I later found out was Joe, tapped me on the shoulder and asked if I wanted a ticket to see a free movie that was going to start in a few minutes.

I didn't say yes, but asked, "Did you say *free*?"

He said, "Yes, and there's free cookies and Kool-Aid in my tent; help yourself."

My throat was parched, and my tummy was growling, so I took Joe up on his offer for free goodies and a movie. He gave me a ticket, and I headed for his tent. I ate some cookies, had some Kool-Aid, and shortly after that, I heard an announcement. The movie was going to start in a few minutes. I went up a few steps into what seemed like a bus—it was a mobile chapel. I saw a screen up front, a projector in the back, and several other children sitting in the seats that were provided. Joe had a couple adult helpers to run the projector, play the music, and adjust the lighting.

Joe got up to speak. He was fun to listen to. I felt good while he told funny stories and talked about Jesus. He had me laughing, and I had not laughed all day. Then he showed us a short movie clip about Jesus. After the movie, Joe got back up. What he was about to say was a life changer for me. Joe reiterated that Jesus loved me so much that he died for me on a cross. He talked about how Jesus rose from the dead. I had heard about Jesus from the Salvation Army ladies that picked me up from school and from my Sunday school teacher with the flannelgraph figures.

Then Joe said the words that changed my life, forever. He asked us if we had ever had a best friend. Then he asked if we *needed* a best friend, a Savior, a Lord, Jesus—a friend that would stick closer than a brother and would never leave me or forsake me. Something inside of me at that very moment was screaming, *Yes! I need a friend like that!*

> What a good decision I had made that day—the decision to trust Jesus.

Joe invited everyone that needed a friend, Savior, and Lord to raise their hand. I raised mine, and a few others raised their hands too. Then he invited all those who had raised their hand to stand to their feet and come to the front of the chapel. That day I quickly made my way to the front of that mobile chapel to ask Jesus to be my best friend, Lord, and Savior, forever. I began trusting in

Jesus that very day for my salvation. Doing so changed the trajectory of my life, eternally.

I guess hearing so much about Jesus and salvation was surprisingly like fishing that first time with Dad. He'd given me so much information that I hadn't been sure I was getting it all. In the front of that mobile chapel, we were also given a lot of information, but didn't understand everything. I trusted the knowledge I understood. That day I was introduced to another dimension in my life: a spiritual one. The Holy Spirit now lived in me. Over time, I began to understand more and more and to recognized what a good decision I'd made that day—the decision to trust Jesus.

Earning Trust

I desire to be reliable, truthful, and trustworthy, but I haven't always lived up to that aspiration. I have lied, cheated, stolen, and demonstrated pridefulness, to name a few of my transgressions. Everyone has sinned and fallen short of God's glory, including me. As long as we live in the flesh, we will struggle with temptation and sin. Even the apostle, Paul, did not understand why he did the things he did not want to do, and why he did *not* do the things he *wanted* to do. We all have the same battle. I don't understand it either, because I always desire to do what is right.

When Dad caught that first fish, I was sort of happy for him, but to be honest, it was a selfish happiness. I was only happy because I believed that I would catch one next. I know that was a small issue, but it was an indication of a larger problem. I'm glad God is merciful and that he's forgiven me.

Dad trusted me enough to take me fishing when I was only five years old. I'm sure taking me was extra work for him. He had to teach me everything, answer all of my questions and help me with just about everything as well. As that was my first time fishing, I did not know much of anything. I appreciated his patience with me and his sacrifice even more after I took my friend's son fishing. Little Bobby was just four years old. I prepared his pole, gave it to him, and told him to, "Throw it in." He walked right up to the edge of the water and threw the pole as far out into the lake as he could. He threw the pole, reel, bobber, hook, everything out

> Ninety-nine percent obedient is disobedient in disguise.

about three feet from shore. Little Bobby did exactly what I had asked him to do. Oh, how patient my dad must have been with me.

I hadn't tried to throw my pole in, but I had tried to do what Dad had told me to do. His trust increased when I did what he asked. I was far from perfect, but he did not expect perfection. He just wanted me to listen, obey, and not give up. I didn't realize it back then, but I was gaining Dad's trust moment by moment.

At times, my faithful obedience is not very faithful or obedient. Instead, I am less trustworthy.

In those early years, Dad didn't talk to me much about the ninety-nine times I'd been obedient. He needed to talk to me about the one time I disobeyed. The more often I was obedient, the stronger trust became.

Faithfulness is like that too. Ninety-nine percent faithful equals unfaithful. My wife would not agree to anything less than complete faithfulness. We build trust and faithfulness moment by moment. It takes a long time to build trust. Trust is built slowly, but can be destroyed in a moment. I want to be trusted, even though I am imperfect in many ways. I need God to lead and guide me and help me make decisions that do not compromise trust. Every one of us is a work in progress. None of us have yet arrived in a glorified state. We are in the flesh and live by and need His grace. Not until we carry out our last deed here on Earth and breathe our last breath will we be in glory.

A person doesn't demonstrate they can be trusted by saying, "I can be trusted." They do it by being trustworthy. I learned to trust myself, my dad, and others at our fishing spot on the Olentangy River. I learned to trust God a few years later at a county fair in Ohio. Today, I seek to live life in a way that allows others to trust me. I am not perfect and never will be in this flesh as my journey is not over. I journey on toward that which only God can someday perfect in me. May the Lord find me faithful.

Discussion Questions

1. Who do you trust? What limitations, if any, do you put on that trust? What makes the people you trust, trustworthy?
2. Do you trust yourself and your abilities? How do you know you can trust yourself? In what areas do you think people have trouble trusting you? Explain your answer.
3. Do you trust God? Do any moments come to mind when you trusted God and He proved to you that you could trust Him? Has He answered your prayers? Has He been a protector? Has He been your provider? Has He been a friend? Has He been a healer? What else has He been to you?
4. Without naming names, relate a time when someone broke their trust. How did you find out? What did you do? Has this person regained your complete trust? If so, how did they do that? If not, how could they regain your trust?
5. What things do you think you need to work on to be trustworthy?

Prayer

Father in heaven, my prayer is that you would find me faithful. Help me in my struggle to say, do, and be the things that I should be. Help me to be a good and faithful spouse, parent, and friend. Father, teach me your ways and help me live in them. Show me my abilities and capabilities and teach me to trust who you caused me to be. I put my trust in you afresh this very moment. Fill me with your love, hope, joy, and peace, and give me faith that remains strong. I pray this in Jesus's special and holy name, Amen.

Launch Team Comments

I've worked at a job I hated, but when my wife had surgery, I felt what you described in this chapter. I didn't want to be anywhere but by her side, yet at the same time, I wanted to be anywhere else. The situation was trying, but we got through it together and are better for it. A.O.

When I met my husband, I knew he was the one for me. We went to California to get married because the telephone company where we'd both worked had gone on strike. His uncle and some cousins lived near San Diego. My fiancé wanted us to go to California, where we planned to be married. I said yes, but my mom asked me a question every loving mother would ask: "What if he leaves you out there by yourself?" I told her that I loved and trusted him. I knew in my heart that he would not leave me, and we have been together for forty-eight years. D.W.F.

I have often put my trust in organizations filled with people I love and trust. These organizations aren't perfect because they're full of imperfect people. That means I cannot trust them fully even though I would like to. Those imperfect people seem to be less than one hundred percent honest and trustworthy. Businesses, non-profits, churches, banks, and hospitals all fall short of perfect honesty and faithfulness. W.L.F.

Chapter Seven
Snags, Tangles, and Hang-ups

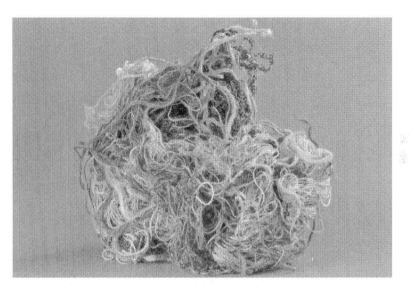

Successfully navigating the snags, tangles, and hang-ups in every facet of life requires real talent. To do this with a Christlike character is much better than with the kneejerk reaction many people have. As a child, I would rely on my parents to help me tackle snags, tangles and hang-ups in life. Today, I am surrounded by wise friends and family that help me make good decisions. My best guide, however, for handling the snags, tangles, and hang-ups of life is the Bible. The Bible teaches that our very best response to any snag, tangle, or hang-up is a Christlike one.

8We are hard pressed on every side, but not crushed; perplexed, but not in despair; 9persecuted, but not abandoned; struck down, but not destroyed. [2 Corinthians 4:8-9]

6Do not be anxious about anything, but in every situation, by prayer and petition, with thanksgiving, present your requests to God. 7And the peace of God, which transcends all understanding, will guard your hearts and your minds in Christ Jesus. [Philippians 4:6-7]

Snags in the River of Life

The Dead End-Road was north of the Delaware Dam on the Olentangy River. At the bottom of the Olentangy River are fallen trees, rocks and other debris causing snags, tangles and hang-ups to be more probable than possible.

One summer day, as we were fishing, my line became snagged on some unseen object in the water. This object had a strong grip on my line, and although I pulled really hard, I could not free it. Not only was my line stuck, but I had a dilemma. I'd reached a snag because I had disobeyed Dad. If I had just listened and obeyed Dad when he told me to stop reeling in my line, this would not have happened. It was my fault.

> We are always at fault for our own disobedience.

Many snags in life happen due to disobedience. I did not want to tell Dad. I'd hoped the line would unsnag itself, but it didn't.

After waiting for what seemed to be a very long time, I'd finally told Dad that my line was snagged. He'd surprised me because he wasn't upset at all. Dad took my pole, pulled it one direction and then the other, and like a pro, he freed my line from the snag. He then cast it out farther than I'd been able to cast, found a forked stick, and set my pole in the Y of the stick. Then he told me to "go and sin no more." No, he didn't say that; he actually told me to watch my bobber until I got a bite.

Coming clean, telling the truth and then moving forward is almost always better than delay, or trying to hide something. A confession indicates honesty which is tougher when we are disobedient. Admitting, "I messed up," "It was all my fault," "I disobeyed," or "I didn't listen" is not natural dialogue for a fallen, sinful person—including a five-year-old boy who thinks he is in big trouble. It's comparable to trying to defend yourself when there is no defense.

If Dad had asked me how my line had gotten snagged, I would have lied. I would have said, "I don't know." That type of response is due to our fallen nature. I had to learn that Dad was not going to explode in anger when I had a snag and needed his help. He may have been disappointed in me, but he never reacted in a harsh way that would have made me want to hide it from him. He never went into an angry fit of rage. Dad made me feel safe to share my snags, tangles, and hang-ups with him.

When I shared my problems with Dad, I learned a few valuable truths about him that spoke highly of his character:

- He enjoyed helping people, and wanted to help me if he could.
- He helped me without yelling, screaming, putting me down, or calling me names.
- He may have lectured me, but he controlled his anger and his tongue.
- He sacrificed to help me and others by giving his time, talents, and treasure.
- He gave out of great love for me and others.
- He was good at figuring things out. He desired to help and was capable.
- He made himself available to me.
- One of his virtues was patience.

I am glad he helped me because there are many snags in the river of life.

Legacy

Many dads aren't around for their young sons. When snags appear, many children have to figure things out for themselves. In some cases, someone else may become a surrogate dad and fill the father role vacancy, such as a grandfather, uncle, pastor, teacher, or coach. The solution is not simply for fathers to be around. The solution is for dads to be engaged in their children's lives. Unfortunately, many dads are more interested in playing video games or entertaining themselves in other ways than they are in spending time with their children.

It is natural for kids to bring their snags, tangles, and hang-ups to their parent or guardian. When they do, parents who listen patiently and respond lovingly reap a great reward. The parent who fails to listen and properly respond will regret not doing so. No matter what the issue—a snag in the carpet, a tear in a curtain, a spilled glass of milk, or something more serious—

if the parent does not stay calm, but goes ballistic, the child may never bring problems to their parent ever again. Explosive responses terrify children and they will find someone else to share with who will listen to them with understanding. But the tragedy occurs when that person fails to have the child's best interest in mind.

I desire and enjoy helping my two daughters. I have often experienced the feeling Dad must have had when he helped me. His way of doing things, who he was and what he stood for—his legacy—lives on. That legacy will continue as my daughters and their husbands parent their children. I've loved being a daddy and am overjoyed to see my children's children. What a treasure they are to me.

Children's children are a crown to the aged, and parents are the pride of their children. [Proverbs 17:6]

My dad was my teacher and taught me how to be a good dad. My job is to teach my children how to be good parents, and their job is to teach their children how to be good parents. This is part of God's plan and passed on as a piece of Dad's legacy. Seeing his legacy alive is a joy. My children's children are my crown. And I am so proud of my parents. Although they are in heaven, much of who they were and how they lived has been passed on to me, and to the following generations. I never thought that one day I would say that I've become like my Dad.

Tangles That Hurt

Every hook inside our tackle box had a very sharp tip. If the tip of a hook touched anything penetrable, it was going in. A short distance from the tip of the hook was a little barb that stuck out, so when the hook went in, it wouldn't come out very easily. When it penetrated the side of a fish's mouth, it was not going to come out very easily. Hooks may easily penetrate, but the exit can hurt a great deal.

Unfortunately, that hook found branches, trees, thorn bushes and a bunch of other stuff. If the hook didn't snag, the line would tangle around it. Dad would generally have to help untangle things so the hook could be free. Sometimes the hook would penetrate my clothing. Disengaging the hook from the fabric may sound easy, but because of the barb, it was difficult to remove.

When the hook had penetrated my skin, it hurt. More than once, I'd yelled, "Dad, get it out! Get it out!" It penetrated my rump, face, arm, back, and hand, and when it did, I needed it removed. It was painful going in, and was often more painful coming out. This principle holds true in life, too. Satan often gets a toe-hold, then a foot-hold, and finally, a stronghold. It is easy to get into a bind, but not so easy getting free. For example, along with drug addictions comes withdrawal. Along with major debt, often comes bankruptcy. Along with abuse, comes separation. Getting into sin brings us pain, but to get out of it almost always hurts more, at least for awhile.

We fished with old open-bail reels. Dad taught me that towards the end of casting my line, I needed to place my thumb on the reel to make it stop spinning. If I didn't do that, I would experience backlash and the reel would become a tangled mess. I am very experienced at causing a tangled-up mess. It would take a long time to untangle the line. I couldn't do it, so I took it to my dad, who would untangle it. I learned that untangling a mess takes a lot longer than creating it.

> Untangling a mess takes a lot longer than creating it.

I hated to bother him about the tangles all of the time, so one day I had a brilliant idea. When the reel backlashed and I had a real mess, I would ignore the tangle. I'd thrown my line out quite a distance into the water. I figured enough line was out in the water that I could cover up the tangled mess by simply reeling the line in on top of the mess. When I reeled my line in on top of the tangled line, to my surprise, the mess *was* entirely covered up. *It worked!* I'd thought.

I cast my line in again, and it backlashed and tangled again. I ignored it again and reeled in the line to cover *that* mess. I did this several times. When I finally took it to Dad, he asked me repeatedly, "What did you do, Son?" When I told him that I'd ignored the first tangle, he made quite a profound statement: Tangles always get worse when we ignore them and try to cover them up.

> Tangles always get worse when we ignore them and try to cover them up.

Distracting Hang-Ups

Dad often placed my fishing pole in a forked stick. He told me to keep my eye on it and wait for a bite. I'd watch it for what seemed a long time. When boredom set in, I'd find other things to do. The river bank had plenty of action, and I was full of energy. I would transform a long stick into a mighty sword. A fallen tree could magically become a saddled horse, and I would straddle it for a ride. Once in a while, I would glance at my pole in the forked stick, and sure enough, it was still there. I could play in the mud, walk the trunk of a tree pretending it was a tightrope. I could skip rocks on top of the water, slide down the path of transition and catch bugs and butterflies. One of my hang-ups was easily becoming bored. I needed action, so I always found something to do.

In the middle of all the fun, dad would tell me to check the bait on my line. I was always happy to oblige him because I wanted the fish to bite too. Each time he asked me to do this, I discovered something different about my bait. Sometimes the bait, hook, line, etc. were fine. Other times, the bait had wiggled partway off the hook and needed adjustment. Sometimes, I realized that something had stolen my bait. I should've been watching. Occasionally, a fish would swallow the bait *and* the hook which would mean it would now be deep inside the fish. Dad always reminded me to watch my pole.

One day, the fish didn't seem to be biting, so I walked away from my pole for a little playtime on the path. As I was playing, I turned to glance at my pole and could not believe my eyes: the bobber was rapidly moving up and down. I ran to my pole, watching the line get tight and straight as an arrow. I made it to the pole just in time to see it pulled over the forked stick and into the water. I had trouble getting my voice to work, but as soon as I did, Dad was in motion. The last time I saw my fishing pole, it was heading downstream at a very fast rate. Dad tried following it, but it eventually went under the water and disappeared forever.

I was no longer bored. I should have been watching my pole and thought I was in big trouble. Shortly after all that excitement died down, we packed up and went home. I didn't have a pole anymore because of boredom. My hang-up had caused us to hang it up for the day. Dad didn't yell or scream at me. In fact, he loved telling the story to friends and relatives. He would laugh as he told them about the day the pole got away. In time, I learned to laugh at the story too.

Breaking Free

Many snags in life can hold people back. Numerous snags are a result of our disobedience. We often believe that there's no way out of the situation. We find ourselves in a dilemma because we don't own it, confess it, and be honest about it. The other factor in the dilemma is not surrendering it to God. He is the only one that can help us, but He will not do that if we hide it. Part of having free will means that we are free to choose to accept God's help or not. When we do, an infinite, all-knowing, all-loving, ever-present, and all-powerful Father in heaven is there as our helper. He will help us break free of our snags, tangles, and hang-ups. All we need to do is ask.

Discussion Questions

1. We all hit snags in our life which can hold us back. Why is this true? Is something holding you back? How many of your snags have occured because of your disobedience?
2. Do you have a hard time admitting when you are wrong or have messed up, or saying that you're sorry for something you did? Do you think our sinful nature gets in the way of true honesty? What is the solution to getting free from the snags of life?
3. Becoming tangled up with something painful is similar to the snags described in this chapter; explain how that is true. Why is it painful and easy to get *into* a tangled-up mess yet much more painful and difficult to get *out* of it?
4. We hide things in closets, drawers, and backrooms so people won't see a literal mess. When we try to hide other kinds of messes in life, what happens?
5. We all have hang-ups—for example, boredom, laziness, timidity, etc.—that can cause us to focus on the wrong things. Awareness of our hang-ups will help us deal with

them. Are you aware of any hang-ups in your life? How do you think God would want us to approach our hang-ups?

6. Many parents today have gone AWOL. Why is this increasing in our society? How are parents sometimes present but not involved? How can we help children live a fuller life by becoming a surrogate dad figure or mom figure? Other than your own mom or dad, did another significant adult help you as a child with your snags, tangles, and hang-ups? Describe that person.

Prayer

God in heaven, you are our Father that will never leave us. We thank you for being with us and helping us with our snags, tangles, and hang-ups. We confess to you that we have them and we need your help to set us free. Forgive us for not coming to you sooner with sincerity and truth. We do not deserve your forgiveness, but you are a God of mercy and grace. We thank you for being willing to forgive. We pray for this generation whose morality and character has appeared to slide. Show us, Father, how we can have the greatest influence. Godly men and women, and moms and dads, are vital to help this generation get back on a Christlike path. Help us, dear Lord, because we need you. We pray in Jesus's name. Amen.

Launch Team Comments

I can't comment very much on growing up with a dad. I was one of the unfortunate ones who grew up without the love and direction of a father. I moved around a lot from several different homes in my formative years, so I had to learn a lot on my own. I had to make some decisions in life without the good counsel of a father. As a result, I believe I understand the difficulties and challenges of other young children growing up without the love of a parent. B.E.

My dad died, and an abusive music teacher became part of my life. Tangles—yes! Snags—yes! Emptiness—yes! Destructive behavior—yes! I hated phony church people who talked a good talk but left my family, who were well known in the community, to go it alone. Mom raised my sister and me. Who led me to Jesus? Would you believe that God did? He gave me a dream. He led me to audition to play drums in a Christian group, and soon I wanted to be like them. My wife was in the group. Your book is both meaningful and painful. God grant you favor as you continue through the process. May He use your book of life lessons with your father to bring men closer to our Heavenly Father. N.B.

We took a boy in and gave him a good home. He was my husband's nephew. My husband could relate to him because he understood his background. The boy seemed to respect my husband but became rebellious and left our home. We are praying for him to have victory over the snags, tangles, and hang-ups in his life. L.A.

This topic hits home. I have a great dad who has been there for me through everything. He has helped through my childhood, sports, marriage, and divorce. He loves my kids like they were his own. He does so much for my family and me; it just goes without saying how blessed we are. And now, while trying to do the same thing for my kids, I understand a lot of the struggles that he probably went through. It is eye-opening when you can finally see the world through your own father's eyes. P.O.

Chapter Eight

Lures, Lies, and Location

Just as fish become enticed, drug away, lured and tempted by what they see, sense, and savor—men, women, boys and girls can be as well. We are enticed to sin by our five physical senses. Sin looks good, smells good, tastes good, sounds good, and feels good. If it didn't, we wouldn't be attracted to it. The pricetag of sin is high and it costs more than we would ever want to pay. Sin always leads us to a lower quality of life than we would want to live.

> The benefit from sin is a temporary pleasure at best, while the cost of sin is high.

12Blessed is the one who perseveres under trial because, having stood the test, that person will receive the crown of life that the Lord has promised to those who love him. 13When tempted, no one should say, "God is tempting me." For God cannot be tempted by evil, nor does he tempt anyone; 14but each person is tempted when they are dragged away by their own evil desire and enticed. 15Then, after desire has conceived, it gives birth to sin; and sin, when it is full-grown, gives birth to death. [James 1:12-15]

The Lure of Big

When Dad had opened the tackle box to get a bobber out, I'd just been amazed at all the neat stuff in there. Hooks, sinkers, bobbers, a wide variety of lures, spinners, shysters, rubber worms, and multiple artificial baits. The colors were fantastic, and the various types and sizes of lures were remarkable. The tackle box became a lure for me because I wanted to go through it and see more. After he'd grabbed the bobber, he closed the tackle box. Clearly, he was not going to let me go through it.

If I had chosen a lure to fish with during that first look in the box, it would have been the biggest lure in the box. I rationalized that if I used the biggest lure, I would catch the biggest fish. What I didn't know was that the biggest lure was as big or bigger than the fish we were going to catch. Dad then told me we were going to fish with live bait anyway.

I have often gone after the biggest, shiniest, and fanciest things in life, which reflects my choice of the biggest lure at first sight. Truthfully, that big lure would not have worked well for me. Choosing it because of its size would have been a mistake. I've also made the mistake of choosing the biggest steak, biggest car, biggest tent, biggest barbecue grill, etc. *Big* is a lure I must be careful of. Big often costs more, and does not always satisfy. Similar to the lure, *Big* may not even prove to be advantageous.

The lure of *Big* is often deceptive. When this type of lure catches my eye, I'm too quick to buy into it. One day not long ago, my wife, Dottie, and I decided to walk through a furniture store. We thought, there's no harm in looking, right? While in the store, I spotted a huge leather sectional sofa set that I loved. The price was right because this particular model was on clearance. They only had one set and I told Dottie that we should buy it right now because at this price it would not last long. Dottie agreed, and we bought the sectional for the fireplace room in our home. When the sectional was delivered a couple of days later, we were very excited. It was going to look great! Unfortunately, It didn't look great—it didn't even fit the room. We were both pretty upset about it.

Because the sofa had been on clearance, we couldn't take it back. We were stuck with it. Even after removing an entire piece of the sectional, it barely fit into the space. It looked terrible because it crowded our fireplace room. We didn't like it at all, but we were stuck with it.

I am a slow learner and am prone to make the same mistake again and again and again. I have learned that big comes in many categories: big size, big name, big price, big opportunity, and big sensation. Yes, the lure of big is a hard one to shake.

Bigger does not equal better.

As I fished with Dad, I learned the biggest minnow didn't catch the biggest crappie. The biggest thermos didn't contain the best beverage. Instead, it contained Dad's black coffee—big but not better. A big salary will not make me rich; a big title will not earn me respect; and a person with a big, important reputation does not make a friend. Bigger does not equal better.

The Lure of Curiosity

I learned from Dad that a simple flash of light reflected from a lure could attract a fish enough for the fish to attack it. Many lures reflect the light and are highly effective at catching fish. One of my favorites is a small, silver spoon lure. It is very enticing, especially to largemouth bass, and many have attacked this lure as it glides through the water. Is curiosity what catches the fish? That must be part of it. Likewise, curiosity persuades us to do things that we normally would not do.

I was attracted to that tackle box, not because of a flash of light, but a flash of sight. I had only caught a few glimpses inside of the tackle box. When Dad opened it, different things would catch my eye, and I was very curious about them. The truth is, I wanted to have a longer look. I wanted to handle those lures and see how they looked up close. I knew they weren't mine—

they belonged to Dad. If he'd wanted to protect me from what was inside the tackle box or even if it were to keep me out of it, that was his prerogative because it belonged to him.

My problem was that every time I got a glimpse, I wanted to see more. My curiosity continued to grow. At one point, my curiosity had grown so much that I felt like I *had* to see more. Curiosity, when it grows, can be dangerous and can alter good judgment.

I began to think differently to justify what I was about to do. Maybe looking in the tacklebox wouldn't be disobeying. Dad didn't say I couldn't look. He said he would explain it later, but if I looked, he wouldn't have to explain it later. I rationalized and talked myself into opening the tackle box. I was beginning to think the tacklebox was partly mine anyway. Dad did call it "our tackle box."

This negative side of curiosity with the lure of that tacklebox was about to get me into trouble, and I hadn't even realized it. I began to believe that no one would ever know. Dad was working, and Mom was in the house. She'd told me I could play in our fenced back yard and inside the garage. There it

> It became an obsession. I had to see more.
> I had to touch it.
> I had to handle it.
> I had to disobey.

was, the tacklebox, sitting on the floor of the garage. I needed to look inside. I knew in my heart that Dad would not approve. Well, *maybe* he would. During this time all alone in the garage, a war between good and evil was going on inside of me. Good was telling me, "You know you shouldn't open the tackle box." Evil was saying, "Go ahead, nobody will ever know." I chose evil and opened the box.

Understanding the principle of good and evil in curiosity is significant. I knew immediately I'd done wrong. It was easy for me to understand why Dad was not excited about me getting inside the tackle box. Within a few minutes, hooks were sticking my little fingers. It hurt, but I dared not cry. I was in big trouble, and I knew it. Ouch, ouch, ouch is just about all I can say about that evil box. I finally got myself free from the hooks and shut the tacklebox without anyone knowing about it. I felt so dirty— and then I had this thought: *Everybody is going to find out.*

Later, Dad came home and pulled the car into the garage. He'd seemed to take longer than normal to come in the house. I thought to myself, *He knows.*

I confessed everything to my dad. I told him I'd been in the tackle box. I told him that the hooks stuck me several times, but I was okay. I also told him I was truly sorry, and would never do that again. Dad and Mom gave me a stern warning, then it was behind us. At that moment, I did not care if I ever opened that evil tackle box ever again.

Curiosity also has a good and healthy side. Every teacher knows the value of curiosity and teaching the curious mind. One of my launch team members, Gail, knows the value of curiosity and uses it very effectively in her teaching. She's taught preschool children in the church and used their curiosity to hold their attention and teach them biblical truth. She wears an apron with over a dozen pockets in it as she teaches, and draws the children's attention to the pockets.

She would tell the students, "In this pocket, is something I know is going to put a smile on your face. In a moment, I am going to show it to you. I wanted to make everyone smile today, so that's why I picked this very special surprise to share with you. It's right here in this pocket. What color do you think it might be? Does anyone want to guess what it is?" The kids would beg her to show them what she had in her pocket. They had to see and had to know. Gail understands that an important part of teaching children is bringing them to the point of discovery where they must see and must know the answers.

Going Where They Are

A variety of species of fish are found in the Olentangy River: bass, catfish, bluegills, carp, crappie, sunfish, and others. They're all good swimmers, fun to watch, and fun to catch. All these fish have both similarities and differences. Some have scales and some don't. Bluegills have a small mouth and are tenacious fighters. They're skilled at stealing the worm right off the hook. Crappies grab live minnows. You'll need to catch several to make a meal, but they're excellent eating. Bass often strike fast and if you're not ready, they will get away with your bait. Fishing for bass can give you an adrenalin rush and excitement galore. Catfish are usually on the bottom of the river because they are bottom feeders. We often fished for them with nightcrawlers after the sun went down at night. Carp seemed to stay in the shallow water at the bottom and some of them were huge. Dad said they weren't good fish to eat but I found out many people do eat them.

We caught all these fish using different lures, live bait, and techniques. Some were bottom feeders which wouldn't normally be attracted to a floating bait. When we fished for bottom feeders, we wouldn't use bobbers. Bobbers would have made the bait float two to four feet below the surface of the water. Instead, we used lead sinkers that would take the line to the bottom of the river. Catfish and other bottom feeders would find the bait there. To catch any particular species of fish, you must go to where they are.

If you've ever hit bottom in your life, you know that it takes someone or something to meet you where you are to help you up. My wife and I have ministered to many people that have hit bottom. I would not have been able to help and minister to them if I hadn't gone to where they were. To reach the poor and disenfranchised people in third-world countries, missionaries have to travel to where these people live. To tell all people about Jesus, we must do what He commanded us to do: Go into all the world and preach the Gospel.

Not too long ago, I traveled with a group from my church to Haiti. We provided Haitian children with shoes, clothes, food, and medicine, and shared the hope that we have in Jesus. We sang with them, washed their feet, laughed with them, worshiped with them, and did what we could to be a blessing for them. We received unexpected blessings, as well. For example, three little girls performed a dance they had practiced for us. While I was there, a realization came over me that those people were very much like me, but their circumstances were very different. Our entire team could have stayed in our country instead of going to Haiti, but we would never have been able to serve as a blessing in the way that we did. We had a real desire to be a blessing to them and to do that, we had to go where they were.

We cannot reach the carp and catfish by fishing on top of the water. We must drop the bait to the bottom, where they are. Fish who feed on the bottom of the river are different from fish who are found nearer to the top. Likewise, people at various social-economic levels and cultures differ from one another, but we all have the same primary need: Jesus.

Discussion Questions

1. Has the enemy, Satan, ever whispered this lie to you: "Go ahead, nobody will ever know," when you were lured away and tempted to sin?
2. After you followed the lure, took the bait, and sinned in your heart, has the enemy ever told you, "Everybody knows"?
3. Why does the enemy use these two lies? Do they work?

4. Explain your understanding of the lure of *Big* and the lure of *Curiosity*. How often are you sidetracked from things God has purposed for you to do in pursuit of big or while chasing something out of curiosity? How can the pursuit of safety, wealth, ease, or anything else, become a lure? What other lures are difficult for you personally?

5. The tackle box was a physical, visible lure. Those types of lures are the ones we feel we must see, touch and explore. Would you consider that type of desire as lust? What are some things, both good and bad, that people lust after?

6. Catching fish requires skill and knowledge. One of the basic things a successful fisherman must know is to go where the fish are. Fish that feed at the bottom cannot be reached by fishing on the surface. Similarly, to help individuals who have hit bottom, with the hope we have from believing in Jesus, do you believe we need to go where they are or wait for them to come to us? What about those that are well educated? What about the wealthy and powerful? What about someone of a different nationality or of a different faith? Or with a different sexual orientation? How can we reach them?

Prayer

Father in heaven, forgive us for chasing the bait of sin and succumbing to the lure that moves us away from righteousness. Help us, Father, to choose right over wrong. Help us to be strong and to rely upon you. Lord protect us from the trickery of evil so that we will do what's right. We pray that our longing for the *biggest* will not deter us from the best. May we not be moved by greed or fame to do what is unrighteous. Lord, we need your help. We pray for those less fortunate than we are. Help us to remember to go where we can be a blessing. Give us the means to go to the poor and the disenfranchised. We love you, Lord. Forgive us where we have failed. In Jesus's name we pray. Amen.

Launch Team Comments

When I was a young child, my Dad would put the loose coins he had in his pocket in a little tray on the dresser. Seeing that change was tempting. One day I decided to steal the change and put it in my pocket. Something was telling me Dad would never know. A day or so later, Dad said he wanted to talk to me about something. Immediately I thought, *He knows.* I confessed every last detail to him. I never found out whether he knew what I'd done or not. W.L.F.

When our daughter was in early gradeschool, her teacher called late in the evening to tell us that she believed our daughter had taken her car keys and had hidden them in her desk. The teacher hadn't been able to go home until she found her keys. My husband and I defended our daughter and said we didn't think she had stolen the keys. If she had, why would she have hidden them in her desk? After denying she took the keys for more than an hour, we told her we believed her, but her teacher did not. We told her that to prove her innocence, we would take her to the home of a police officer we knew, and he would give her a lie detector test. Our daughter immediately confessed. W.F.

Conversion vans were very popular when our motor home was developing a lot of problems. We began to explore buying a conversion van, even though they were very expensive. I found a brand-new GMC van with a Coachman conversion. It was the best of the best at that time. We still owed about $5000 on the motor home, but the Pontiac dealership said they would offer us a good deal on the conversion van. I was so starry-eyed, wanting this van they used as a lure, that I signed a ten-year loan to buy it. The payments were high, and vans rarely lasted ten years. This van did last ten years, but I regretted buying it. It was way too expensive. The lure was big, and I fell for it. T.P.P.

Chapter Nine
Responding to Difficulties

Living a joy-filled Christian life does not mean you won't experience times of difficulty and times when you wish you could be somewhere else. No one likes discomfort, discouragement, or pain, but all of these things are a part of every person's life. Our response to the best and worst times is what makes life either a perpetual nightmare or a perpetual joy. I have chosen perpetual joy, and its completeness is in Jesus Christ, my Lord and Savior.

> Our response to the best and worst times is what makes life either a perpetual nightmare or a perpetual joy.

7Cast all your anxiety on him because he cares for you. 8Be alert and of sober mind. Your enemy the devil prowls around like a roaring lion looking for someone to devour. [1 Peter 5:7-8]

35Who shall separate us from the love of Christ? Shall trouble or hardship or persecution or famine or nakedness or danger or sword? 36As it is written: "For your sake we face death all day long; we are considered as sheep to be slaughtered." 37No, in all these things we are more than conquerors through him who loved us. 38For I am convinced that neither death nor life, neither angels nor demons, neither the present nor the future, nor any powers, 39neither height nor depth, nor anything else in all creation, will be able to separate us from the love of God that is in Christ Jesus our Lord. [Romans 8:35-39]

The Best and the Worst

There was so much to love about the Dead-End Road. The Olentangy River ran through the countryside and was everything a young boy would ever want. It was an adventure, a challenge, and yielded many rewards, sometimes a stringer of fish.

The picturesque setting would make an artist's canvas come alive. The huge trees that lined the river were a canopy of beauty and shade, and their shadows moved with the wind. The noises resembled an orchestra as it warms up before the concert. The sounds did not blend together as a well-organized symphony would. The only constant sound was the river crashing on the shoreline with a booming splash and quiet retreat. Other sounds interrupted the quietness: a bird suddenly singing its song, a squirrel disturbing the fallen leaves as it ran underneath the trees, an unexpected scary screech of an owl, a car door slamming up by the road, or a cow mooing in a distant pasture. These interruptions created this amazing setting, wonderful and indescribable for me as a little boy.

All these things are just a memory now, but I can still close my eyes and imagine them happening all around me. I must be careful, though, as I remember what I loved so much about the Dead-End Road because I truly remember it as a wonderful overall experience. The truth is, after summing everything up— the good plus the bad plus the painful plus the joyful—when I hit the equal key, the totality of the experience was very positive and very fun.

The adventure that I loved, however, included things that I didn't like. When I'd experienced these unpleasant things for a moment, I did not want to be there.

At the Dead-End Road, there were very few things that I wouldn't have at least tried or attempted. Sometimes a task was too difficult and I would ask for help, but most of the time, I tried to take care of it myself. On my first trip to the Dead-End Road, after we were somewhat settled, I needed to use the bathroom. I couldn't see any bathrooms or porta-potties, nothing. I did not want to be somewhere without bathrooms, but I also did not want to go home. I'm sure I held it until I couldn't anymore. I was thinking we would have to haul all our stuff back to the car and find a bathroom. Out of desperation, I finally told Dad I had to go. He told me if I had to pee, use a tree. Call me naive, but at the time, I could not figure out how a tree would help the situation. After Dad had explained it to me, what a tremendous relief it had been to empty my bladder.

Almost every time we went to the Dead-End Road, I experienced something that made me not want to be there. For example, I saw snakes in the water and on the riverbank. I didn't want to be anywhere near those snakes. Once, I pulled some weeds around a tree. By the time Dad discovered what I'd been pulling, it was too late. He told me it was poison ivy. Poison? I didn't want to be there. One day while we fished, I noticed what looked like a little black cloud moving around near the river. Dad told me it was a swarm of bees, and said if they started our way, to run for safety. Bees?! At that moment, I did not want to be there.

A little rain never hurt anyone, so when it rained, I was hoping Dad wouldn't say, "Let's pack it up." We patiently waited as the rain steadily increased. Soon, a crack of thunder shook the very ground we were fishing from. Lightning lit up the sky around us. Dad said, "Grab your stuff, and run." When I heard that crack of thunder, it scared the bejeebies out of me, and I did not want to be there. We went home that day soaking wet and miserable. I was so cold and did not warm up until my mom wrapped me in a huge warm towel and hugged me for a little while.

One day as we walked on the path of activity, I stepped into what had looked like a little mud puddle, but to my surprise, was not a puddle at all. I sank into cold water up to my thigh. Dad had to help me out of that hole. My shoe, sock and pant leg were wet, and I was cold. I did not want to be there at that moment. It didn't take long though to dry out in the morning sun, and then I was once again glad to be there.

Yes, there were moments when I did not want to be at the Dead-End Road, but those times were few compared to all the adventure and fun that I shared with my Dad. Perspective was key. For many of us, our perspective slants toward the positive. Others' perspectives are slanted toward negative experiences. It becomes a choice.

Obstacles are Temporary

Every day that I live is a mix of wonderful times and difficult times. The mix is experienced with good and bad people, with ease and difficulty, and with energy and fatigue. Life is an everyday mix of many things. But, hope that endures no matter what happens makes a positive difference. If hope becomes depleted, it is impossible to have a positive attitude.

Hope helps me to remember the good times, my life purpose, my goals, the people who love me, and that obstacles are temporary. Remembering these things has made my life much grander. That is why I choose to remember them well. I am less apt to remember and dwell on the negative things of life because I know those memories would make me bitter and angry.

Sometimes, when I need to be where I am, I do not want to be there. For example, when my mother's doctor had told us that he was very sorry but he had diagnosed my mother incorrectly. The cancer was back, and had advanced to the liver. At that moment, a sickening feeling came over me, and I did not want to be there—but I'd needed to be. This family moment was very difficult for all of us.

When our youngest daughter was born, the doctor had told us that our little girl had respiration problems and was going to be placed in an incubator to help her breathe. Somewhere during the conversation, the doctor had said she might not make it as her chances of survival were about fifty percent. I remember that sick hurting feeling I'd had in my heart. I did not want to be there, and I did not want to hear that news, but I had to. One effect this had was to improve my prayer life. I began praying with my wife that day. I realized the power of communal prayer too. I believe our daughter was healed during the hour our church had been praying at an altar rail especially for her. She is now married, has two children, and is in my book launch team.

My wife had attempted to do something helpful and clean out our fireplace so that I wouldn't have to. Her motive and intent were sincere, but the result was not what she had expected. We had replaced our carpet in front of the fireplace, and she was careful to keep the bucket on the stone hearth. After she had spent about an hour cleaning all the ash out of the fireplace, she picked up the bucket to take it outside.

I wish I could stop telling this story right at this point, but in reality, when she'd picked up the bucket, the bottom fell out. The bucket was plastic and she admitted she hadn't thought of that. The ash spilled on the new carpet, some of it still smoldering. Seeing the burn spots on the carpet, she felt terrible. Now, she would have to tell me about it.

I also wish I could tell you I'd taken it in stride and was a comfort to her troubled heart, but I'd lost my cool. I'd become hotter than the ash, and I know that I screamed at her. It would be fair to say that the things that came out of my mouth were not very well thought out. My tongue got way ahead of my brain, and I made a complete fool of myself.

After I'd said it all, I began to feel bad and got that little sick feeling in my heart. I felt God was talking to me like a father lovingly correcting a son, "Do not lose your home over a few burn spots in the carpet." Ouch! I thought about this and tried with all my heart to apologize and make things right with her, and I know I finally succeeded. But I will never forget this incident because when I realized what I had done, I did not want to be there. I was so sorry and still am.

Not too long ago, my superintendent told me that I had done a very good job pastoring the church where I had served for twenty years. I had always received good reviews, and without a doubt, the people I'd pastored loved me, and I loved them as well. I had led the church through major financial difficulties, and we'd been able to accomplish some phenomenal things, with God as our helper. The church's Official Board respected my leadership and often told me that I was appreciated. My superintendent, a good friend of mine, met with me and affirmed his appreciation, love, and the excellent job I had done in the church. I had publicly began telling people that I intended to retire in a couple of years. The Minister's Appointment Committee decided it would be in the best interest of the church to appoint a different pastor to the church I was pastoring. Although I'd planned to retire in two years, they'd felt that making a change that year made more sense than waiting two years for me to retire. They believed they had found the perfect replacement.

When the superintendent told me all of this, I did not want to be there; I did not want to hear what he was saying. I was hurt and devastated. My initial thought was not that they were doing something wonderful for me, but *How could they do this to me?* I had that sick feeling in my heart. It was a shock and I needed time to pray about my response. I began to wonder if I had done something wrong or if I had messed up, but I knew I had done my best. It was not a death sentence. I was going to be appointed to another church to conclude my time before retiring. I could have had a fit and yelled and screamed but what would that have changed? It would have changed nothing except how others viewed my integrity and character.

I have always been a man under authority while also a man of authority. Fortunately, I have learned a few lessons since the fireplace incident. I began to see things from the committee's viewpoint, and if they thought this was the best thing for the church, the conference, and me, maybe they were right. Although I wanted to stay, I began to see that this was probably God's way of moving me on to something else I had wanted to do. Otherwise, I would never have moved. I walked away from that church with a great love for the people there, and a great love and respect for those who had authority over me.

In my lifetime, I have found myself in many places where I did not want to be, but I had to be there. It was not easy, but it was always necessary. We can choose whether to believe that or not but Apostle Paul describes it best:

And we know that in all things God works for the good of those who love him, who have been called according to his purpose. [Romans 8:28]

Discussion Questions

1. Discuss a few times in your life when you had to be in a certain situation, but did not want to be. What happened? How did you feel about it then? How do you feel about it now?
2. Have you ever been embarrassed by your own behavior? Has your mouth ever run ahead of your brain? When this

happened, were you able to make things right? Why do you think you remember the incident so vividly?

3. What have you learned about life through the experiences where you wanted to be somewhere else? How aware are you of the times when others are feeling that way?

4. Tell about a time when you realize God had his hand in something you did not want to do, but you had to? How do you know God was orchestrating it?

5. Many people are not where they want to be because they are in bondage. Give examples of people you know who are in bondage to addiction.

6. Can you think of a time when you know you should have been somewhere and weren't? Talk about those times and how things turned out.

Prayer

Father in heaven, we know that you place and lead us. We pray for you to continue to lead and place us where you want us to be. Sometimes you lead us to places, things, and situations that we would never choose. Lord, help us to recognize when it is you that is leading. Help us Lord, to be people of character and integrity. Help us to grow to new heights in every area of our lives. Help us through the tough transitions that we'll have today and in the future. Help us to look for you wherever we are. When we wander to places you do not want us to be, move us back to the place of your will. We love you! In the name of Jesus, I pray this. Amen.

Launch Team Comments

When I was a child, someone hurt me badly. During that time of hurt, I wanted to be anywhere else but there. Praise God that when I was older, I found Jesus. He held me and let me know that I was so loved and cared for by Him. D.W.F.

I worked for a vending and catering company as a cook during the midnight shift. Things were stolen from some of the trucks in the parking lot during the early morning hours. My manager asked if I would walk around the building every hour during my shift to see if I could find out what was going on. I made the rounds at 1:00 a.m. It was dark and pretty scary. What was I thinking when I'd agreed to do that? At 2:00 a.m., I began to walk around the building again, when I heard, "Halt! You, up against the wall!" It was the Mansfield Police Department K-9 Unit. The company had asked the police to watch the building too. They kicked my feet open and frisked me, and a police dog was barking at me. I was in an all-white baker's uniform. Embarrassed and with bruised ankles, I wanted to be somewhere else. It turned out to be a case of mistaken identity. W.L.F.

Chapter Ten

The Desire to Stay on the Mountain

I have often desired to stay where I've found comfort, fulfillment, joy, safety, peace, acceptance, and fun—and why not? The mountaintop is glorious, and I would be crazy to want anything else. God does not take us to the mountain to stay there. He meets with us to prepare us for what's coming next in our lives as He uses us for His glory.

> *¹After six days Jesus took with him Peter, James and John the brother of James, and led them up a high mountain by themselves. ²There he was transfigured before them. His face shone like the sun, and his clothes became as white as the light. ³Just then there appeared before them Moses and Elijah, talking with Jesus. ⁴Peter said to Jesus, "Lord, it is good for us to be here. If you wish, I will put up three shelters—one for you, one for Moses and one for Elijah." ⁵While he was still speaking, a bright cloud covered them, and a voice from the cloud said, "This is my Son, whom I love; with him I am well pleased. Listen to him!" ⁶When the disciples heard this, they fell facedown to the ground, terrified. ⁷But Jesus came and touched them. "Get up," he said. "Don't be afraid." ⁸When they looked up, they saw no one except Jesus. ⁹As they were coming down the mountain, Jesus instructed them, "Don't tell anyone what you have seen, until the Son of Man has been raised from the dead." [Matthew 17:1-9]*

The Temporary Mountaintop Experience

Standing on the high path of contemplation at the Dead-End Road was like standing on a mountain top. From this perspective, I could see the riverbed and all of its surroundings. It was big and beautiful—my childhood mountain.

The busy world of stressed-out adulthood had not left its ugly mark on the Dead-End Road. Dad seemed relaxed and we were able to have a continual father and son talk. Dad worked countless hours, and his responsibilities were huge. The only time available for us to talk at home was during dinner and an hour or so before I went to bed. At the Dead-End Road, I had his attention the entire time, and we talked about all sorts of interesting things.

The day progressed rapidly and soon we were eating lunch and the afternoon hours passed quickly. As evening approached and the sun began sinking lower in the sky, I wished for more time on the mountain. Eventually, Dad said those dreaded words, "Well son, are you ready to pack it up and call it a day?" I was never ready. I always tried to bargain with Dad for more time. Another ten minutes! Then after that, another ten minutes. After using all of my bargaining chips, I sadly pulled my line in, packed up, and headed down the path of activity with Dad, a short distance to the path of transition, then to the high path of contemplation, then to the car. The chatter was nonstop on the way home. When we arrived at our house, I had to tell everyone about our day. It was impossible to describe the mountain top experience exactly the way I had enjoyed it. I tried to tell them about the fish we'd caught and the fish that had gotten away. I could hardly wait to go back to the mountain, the Dead-End Road, again.

Receiving Jesus as my Lord and Savior was a mountaintop experience for me, but I eventually had to come down from the mountain. I had a ministry to accomplish and a life to live. Good times; graduations, ordinations, marriage, honeymoon, and a sabbatical may all qualify as mountain-top experiences, but they are temporary. We cannot stay there. God has work for us to do. We should enjoy the mountain when we are on one, but look for the transition to appear soon.

Mountaintop experiences can be spiritual occasions where we get filled up spiritually. Hopefully, you have enjoyed mountain-top experiences that have provided spiritual fulfillment. I often come back from these experiences with great thanksgiving and praise in my heart. I need to remember when I return from these experiences that I am coming down to people who didn't experience what I just did. They often tend to throw water on the fire we bring down with us. As we come down, we need to ease into the mainstream of life but not forget the clarity of focus we received on the mountain. We don't *want* to come down from the mountain, but we must.

> Mountaintop experiences can be spiritual occasions where we get filled up spiritually.

The mountain was where Moses received his call and the Law (Ten Commandments), and where he received instruction about how to construct the tabernacle. On a mountain, Moses experienced the Glory of God. He had to cover his face because he had been in the presence of the almighty God and people would not be able to safely gaze upon his face.

Descending the Mountain

For Moses, the mountain became a place of contemplation and where he experienced the presence of God. But Moses had to come down to lead the people.

The mountain was also where the transfiguration of Christ took place. Jesus transfigured before three of his disciples. The disciples who were with him watched in jaw-dropping amazement. Jesus and the disciples had to come down from the mountain because Jesus had to finish His work on the cross, and the disciples had to spread the Gospel.

When John baptized Jesus, the Holy Spirit descended on him like a dove. I can imagine that must have been a mountaintop experience for both John and Jesus. But after His baptism, the Bible says Jesus was led into the wilderness by the Spirit to be tempted by the devil.

Often, we need a break from the rat-race of our human experience to be in the presence of God. Sometimes just a break from our work will provide a reprieve from the rat-race; other times we may need a long weekend, vacation, or a trip to a place like the Dead-End Road.

Mountains are a blessing that God provides for us, but He does not intend for us to stay there. When we experience a mountain given to us by God, we experience God in some way. It is no wonder that we do not want to come down. It feels like we are leaving the presence of God. But that is only an illusion; God is always with us. He said He would never leave us and we know His word is true. We do experience Him on the mountain, yet when we begin to descend, he leads us. He has plans for things he wants us to do, and he will be with us.

So why don't we sense God after we descend as we do on the mountain? One reason is because of the larger presence of evil and the enemy when we are off the mountain. Busyness, multiple activities, and tremendous stress draw our attention. Our five senses draw us in so many directions. Our eyes see what we should not see, our ears hear what we should not hear, and so on. God is always there, but we are not always aware of His presence. The result is that we often take our

> Our five senses draw us in so many directions.

eyes off of God, even if we don't want to. Hopefully, recognizing these distractions will lead us to desire a return trip to the mountain to be in God's presence.

Discussion Questions

1. Describe and discuss some of the mountaintop experiences that you've had in your life. What made them mountaintop experiences? Did anyone else experience these with you?
2. Do you think the Dead-End Road was a mountaintop experience for my father and me? Why or why not?
3. When I tried to bargain with my Dad for ten more minutes at the Dead-End Road, did that remind you of any bargaining that you have done?
4. The literal mountains that Moses and Jesus were on were amazing. The presence of God was evident at both. Have you experienced God on your mountains? In what ways?
5. When we come down from the mountain, God desires to lead us. Why is it difficult for us to experience the presence of God?

Prayer

Father in heaven, we thank you for the mountain. We long for your presence even though we know you are always with us. Lord, we get distracted and busy; forgive us. Help us to be mindful of your presence every day. Forgive us when we fail to go the direction you are leading. Open our spiritual senses so we can see things, people, and experiences the way You see them. God, we desire for you to meet us on the mountain and for us to be wise enough to go there when we have to. Thank you, Lord, for the experiences of this book and the simple truths of life. I pray all of this in the precious name of Jesus. Amen.

Launch Team Comments

The mountaintop; I think God's view from above puts mountain tops and valleys on the same level. Flying in an airplane, I can see the ridged landscape but can't tell how far down the valleys go. So many times, I've sat alone in the church and felt his presence. Wanting to stay there for hours, I was nudged to move on to the next task for the day. Time spent there, no matter how long, was never enough. I reflected on the story about when the disciples would come down the mountain and I realized that Jesus had gone with them. What made those moments so special was that Jesus was there. Once I recognized His presence stayed with me, the mountaintop was not a destination but a way of life. D.W.

I had a bad accident and fractured my elbow, and it was not healing right, and I could not straighten it out. One night I went to the altar of our little Free Methodist church in Ocala, Florida. My husband was the pastor, and several other Christ-followers laid their hands on me. They anointed me with oil and prayed for my healing. My arm became strangely warm, and suddenly, I went down. I can't explain it; I just went down. My husband was as surprised as I was. It had never happened in our church before. Some call it "slain in the Spirit." I don't know what to call it, but God was answering my prayer. My arm straightened out. God healed me. I think we all met God on a mountain that night. D.W.F.

One time I was in the basement of my home praying to God for his anointing. It was winter in Ohio and snow had blanketed the area with about six inches of snow. As I was praying and sensing the presence of God, the doorbell rang. I was alone in the house, so I ran to the door. Nobody was there. And the snow on the porch had no footprints in it. I went back to the basement to pray, and the doorbell rang again. I went to the door. Nobody was there and still no footprints. I prayed again, and all of a sudden, I felt a physical sensation of something poured on me, like warm oil being poured on my head and running down my face and shoulders. I believe I was on the mountain. W.L.F.

About the Author

Pastor Bill Fix is married to his wife of forty-eight years, Dottie Winbigler Fix. They have two beautiful married daughters, godly sons-in-law, and four grandchildren. He was a lead pastor for thirty-eight years, serving a total of three churches. He has a doctoral degree in theology and a Master of Religious Education. His hobbies include fishing, hunting, reading, and writing. He loves his family and enjoys entertaining audiences with illusions and ventriloquism to teach about Jesus. He makes his home in Taylor, Michigan.

He serves on the Board of Directors at Community Care Services where he is the past president and current treasurer. Pastor Bill Fix has had the privilege of being the keynote speaker at Light & Life Christian School's high school graduation and gave the invocation for the Wayne County Community College District graduation held at Ford Field three consecutive years. He was also invited to  present the invocation for the Wayne County Executive's State of the County address. He is a member of the Taylor Substance Abuse Prevention Task Force, has served on the Wayne County Interfaith Coalition and has served as an adjunct professor at Spring Arbor University. As The People Pastor, Pastor Bill Fix remains involved in the community that he loves and the family he has been blessed with.

Made in the
USA
Monee, IL